THE HIGHER SELF VOICE
ON

CHOICES

Neutralizing Your Negative Thoughts and Emotional Blueprints

ISBN 978-1-60910-080-3

Printed in the United States of America.

THE HIGHER SELF VOICE
ON

CHOICES

Neutralizing Your Negative Thoughts and Emotional Blueprints

By
Janet Richmond

Acknowledgements

I wish to thank with all my heart the following people: Joel Gotler, a very dear friend, who was the first to request that I write this book. He had the faith that I could do it and his faith sent me on the incredibly exciting journey that gave birth to *CHOICES*. Craig Hilary, another dear friend, stepped up to help me above and beyond any expectation and made the huge commitment to school me on the book writing process. He gave me the gift of his time on a weekly basis for the first half of the book, greatly shortening my learning curve and making it a joyful experience. His encouragement, support and constant editorial help were invaluable. Katherine Pruneda, my assistant and friend, has more capability and competence than I could have ever wished for and her tireless dedication enabled me to bring this book to a level of excellence than it could even have been without her.

Many, many others helped me as well. I thank all of my friends that read endless drafts and gave me essential feedback. I thank Aime McCrory of The Business Muse, someone who gave me time, important marketing and publishing information and referred me to several other professionals that have helped me in many areas. I thank Sheryl Farber, the professional copy editor, whose patience with a first time writer and speed in getting the editing done were valuable pieces of the book process. And I thank Lynne Kastner, whose deep friendship and long-term experience with the Higher Self Voice, gave me insights, tremendous support and valuable feedback on many aspects of the book.

Table of Contents

Author's Preface

Biographical facts would not tell you who I am or who I am becoming. Bottom line: I am part of humanity, experiencing the good, the bad, the ugly and the indifferent of the human condition. There will always be people who are better or worse off than I will.

Like everyone, I have had my own share of challenges. My parents died in a car accident when I was 18 months old. The event left me psychologically and emotionally devastated. I grew up feeling I was in an unsafe world, scared of my own shadow, and I would deliberately blur my eyes when talking to other people. It was the coping mechanism I used even into my teens that enabled me to function despite my shyness. If I couldn't see someone clearly (my childlike thinking went), then other people couldn't really see me either. Hiding was my major defense.

Fortunately, I did have good things going for me, too, including a wonderful adoptive family (my aunt and uncle) and good friends. But my core emotional state made it difficult for me to feel and experience anything positive. I was a basket case.

I could have given up and lived life by coping as best I could and feeling out of control on a daily basis. Fortunately, my misery led to a deep desire to fix myself. I wasn't going to accept my fear, low self-esteem, passivity, crippling shyness, or victim mentality without a fight. I wanted something better from life—more balance, inner peace, meaning, love, and less hurt, struggle, drama and shame. So I began to look for answers.

During my many years of searching to understand myself, I discovered that there were patterns in my life that actually defined and seemed to control me. Each pattern involved its own slew of actions and reactions, which often kept me in a state of self-sabotage. I learned to identify the poor choices I made and why I kept on choosing them. So whenever I screwed up, I was able to say, "Yes…there is that old pattern again." However, I was unable to change those patterns and break out of my ruts. I felt powerless. Even though I had matured in some important ways—becoming a successful business owner and a mother of two wonderful children—I was still unhappy. So the search continued.

The Decision That Changed My Life

In 1983, I went for a psychic reading from Joan Culpepper. I had heard about her from my hairdresser, who went to Joan for regular readings. I'm not sure why I decided to meet her, but it was the decision that changed my life.

Joan was not the kind of person I thought she would be. I was sort of expecting a woman wearing a turban and tie-dyed clothes, who spoke a lingo I could barely understand. Instead, I found a woman in a wacky 'Foxy Lady' T-shirt, drinking a cup of coffee. She quickly put me at ease as she opened up a little about herself. She told me she was from the South and was brought up as a Southern Baptist. She said that her move to Los Angeles opened her eyes. In L.A. she became aware of the metaphysically-oriented information that helped her understand and appreciate the psychic experiences she'd had since childhood. Then, after becoming disillusioned with some of her metaphysical teachers, she decided to take responsibility for acquiring her own information. She soon developed her own gifts and began to conduct psychic readings.

In addition to a Tarot spread, part of Joan's reading included accessing information from the Higher Selves, with what Joan called a soul scan. Joan explained to me that the Higher Selves were more highly evolved soul aspects from the 5th Dimension and from whom she obtained higher-level information. (Though more will be explained in Chapter Two, simply stated, the 5th Dimension is where we all go when we graduate from the Human Kingdom into the next level of evolution.) At first, I didn't really understand what she meant, but I was able to suspend disbelief enough to listen. And I'm so glad I did. The Higher Selves gave me the extraordinarily broad overview of my soul's journey over eons of time. It included what that journey meant for me at that point in my life. It was not a past-life reading. It was an explanation of my soul's evolutionary mission for billions of years. Wow! That got my attention!

Toward the end of the soul scan, the Higher Selves addressed a very real problem for me. For years I'd been experiencing almost daily anxiety, sometimes related to what was going on with me and sometimes having no basis at all. It was not the panic attack variety but an uncomfortable and unwanted loud background noise that rarely let me forget it was there.

The Higher Selves explained to me that anxieties are toxins of the mind. They said that when there are toxins in one's body, the result is often a bout of diarrhea. Of course, since no one holds on to diarrhea, the toxins are released. However, we often mistakenly hold on to the mind's toxins. We worry, we obsess, we lose sleep, we over analyze and we chronically focus on our problems in different ways. The Higher Selves suggested that when I feel anxious, instead of thinking about it, I should do a releasing exercise. I was to visualize the anxiety coming out of the top of my head as black smoke and then turning to white as it hit the air.

I didn't have anything to lose, so I tried it. And sure enough, when I did the exercise, the anxious feelings disappeared almost immediately. In the next couple of days I did it two or three more times. And that was it. No more anxiety. It just went away and didn't come back. The exercise was so simple and yet so effective.

That experience, as well as learning all of the other intriguing things from the Higher Selves in the reading, motivated me to become part of Joan's various metaphysical groups for the next four years. As someone with an extremely analytical mind, I was initially skeptical, even though I'd experienced immediate benefits. However, I soon began to accept that the information was completely practical, consistent and logical, even though it was coming from something, somewhere, and/or someone I couldn't see or touch (the Higher Selves). And its impact was incredible.

Joining Joan's Groups

Since I found myself completely drawn to the information, I began going to Joan's Wednesday-night meeting, her basic meditation group. It exceeded my expectations. This group was called a conscious meditation group. The Higher Selves led the group, talking to us in an informal but informative way. Their goal was to teach us to receive information in the moment, i.e., while we were conscious, and not in the alpha state, as in regular meditation. The Higher Selves explained that while one is in the alpha state, information often comes through in symbols that need to be interpreted once out of the meditative state. This was not the case with conscious meditation. So our journey began.

Every week the Higher Selves brought us exercises geared toward developing our own abilities. A primary goal was to have each of us access the Higher Self information by ourselves and for ourselves. Joan was never meant to be the only one. And it was challenging for me, to say the least. I couldn't even get to what I called "first base"—just feeling the energy of the Higher Selves. Months went by where I felt like I was way behind everyone else. Then one day the Higher Selves said, “If you can’t hear us, just imagine what we would say. Imagination gives you a starting point and will allow you to tune into the stream of contact energy.” That really helped me. It was the start of my opening up to receive their information.

As the weeks went by, the Higher Selves also brought information into the class about how our outer reality is created and how we can recreate it to be what we want it to be. They then supplied the techniques for how to do just that. Because changing my reality was what motivated me from the beginning, I listened intently. I immediately started using the exercises they gave us and worked diligently on them. Now I was getting somewhere! Over time, and after all the work I was doing on my own, I made progress. The fear and insecurity that had held me prisoner for so long began to ease. There was movement at last, and I had the Higher Selves information to thank.

Simultaneous to the Wednesday group, Joan began something called the Entity Group, which involved working with disincarnate humans (people who have died). This started in early 1984 and went on for two-plus years. The group met every three weeks. For someone like me, it was incredible. What drew me in at first was the phenomenon of it—working with souls who had passed intrigued me. What I quickly discovered, though, was how much I could learn from this. It became immediately clear to me that dying did not change the type of person he/she was. If someone was angry and mean in life, he/she was angry and mean after death. If someone was ignorant and prejudiced in life, he/she was ignorant and prejudiced after death. But just as everyone alive has the immense capacity to learn and grow, so do the souls of the deceased. With the Higher Selves help and as a result of the group, that is exactly what happened.

What developed for me from this group experience is that I gained a deeper understanding of what heaven is and what happens when you die. I also began to work on my ability to connect with the dead. Therefore, this group, which we called Jane and Company, was the cornerstone of my understanding death and the evolution of the soul.

My Involvement Expands

In addition to these two groups, Joan also provided other classes, in all of which I participated. These included a 5th Dimensional healing class, a contact group, and a history of the Universe class. On my own I also developed a type of metaphysical energy work I call Catalytic Art.

In an early reading from Joan, the Higher Selves gave me the information and techniques for this type of art. Basically, Catalytic Art is artwork infused with energy that can bring changes to one's life. Conscious thought directs energy into the picture and works slowly but effectively to either move a negative pattern into a more positive place and/or to help create something completely new. Since I initially felt as artistic as a rock—I hadn't done any art since the second grade—this was a process I took on from a place of faith. Yet my inexperience with art turned out to be a positive thing, as this art form is created through a largely unconscious method. Not knowing the normal rules of art technique actually freed me from potential limitations.

For the first two years I tracked every one of my pictures to convince myself that the art's catalytic energy was working. After many examples of positive results, my faith was substantiated. Over the years I have grown and expanded with my artwork. I've even had shows and taught the technique to others. This spiritual artwork has become a fulfilling and important part of my destiny.

A Significant Shift in Focus

In 1987, Joan moved to Tennessee, where her brother lived. She decided to help him with his business and take the time to write her book on the 5th Dimensional story. Joan wanted the Higher Self information to be available to the world. The group was thrilled that she was going off to write her book, and in her absence, we continued accessing all the information on our own in different ways. I spent the next several years working alone and with friends, utilizing, developing and expanding upon what we had learned.

According to the Higher Selves, I was most receptive to the information when outdoors, I learned to tune in to them while jogging or walking. This way, I exercised and did the inner work simultaneously, and it became my favorite time to connect with the Higher Selves. I honed my listening skills and developed an ability to receive information consciously. Self-doubt, which had haunted me from my earliest memories, began to disappear from my life. I went a long way toward healing my fears, and this wallflower stepped away from the wall. It didn't happen overnight, but progress was steady, significant and rewarding.

At some point in the mid 1990s, Joan returned. She moved to Diamond Bar, California, to be near her daughter and her granddaughters. She had not yet written the book, since the demands of her life in Tennessee didn't allow time for it. Upon her return, she began taking care of her grandchildren, still very young at the time. She became busy with that, and despite protests from many of her students, her professional spiritual life basically ended. (For more information on Joan, please see Appendix I.)

Closing in on Present Day

Sometime in 2003 or 2004, I approached Joan to see if there was some way that we could work together to write the Higher Self book. She knew that I had come to absorb, use, and expand upon much of the Higher Self information. Yet, despite our attempts to do it together, there were a series of delays. Then in 2006 Joan died unexpectedly. We were in shock. This woman was a metaphysical genius. She cared for all of humanity and would be greatly missed. She was now on to another phase in her soul's journey.

At Joan's memorial, given by her daughter Trish, many of us came together to honor her, to share our grief and to celebrate her gift to humanity. My appreciation of that gift made me even more determined to make sure that it was not lost. Trish knew her mother would want me to have the Higher Self wisdom that had been preserved on hundreds of cassette tapes. Therefore, she gave me her permission to do what was needed in order to get this knowledge out into the world.

For me, the Higher Self information was the solution to a lifetime's desire for answers and help. This information has been the foundation of my life from the first moment I became aware of it. I live it every day and now see the world through its expanded lens. I discovered that even though some of my issues weren't resolved as quickly as my anxiety problem, my life began to seriously improve with consistent use of the Higher Self information. On some deep level I woke up, fully accepting the concept that my life was my responsibility. With this knowledge came freedom and determination—freedom from the old belief systems that kept me prisoner, and determination to help myself. As I have delved deeper and deeper, eliminating my soul's negative patterns, I have been able to be myself from a place of truth I never knew existed before. Not all readers will go as deeply into this work as I did. But you will benefit from even a small effort. And a little more effort will achieve even more. The potential is there for anyone to tap into at his or her own level.

The Results

I wake up happy every single day. I'm healthier now than I was in my thirties. It doesn't mean that my life is perfect or that problems don't arise. It just means that now my problems don't seem like problems and instead, are opportunities to take additional steps forward. Over the years many of my issues have been resolved, many changes have been made and my mind has been expanded. I am actively creating my life to be what I want it to be, rather than have it happen to me by happenstance. My emotions are no longer leading me around by my nose, and I am becoming more and more of what I always knew I could be, but was unable to reach. I've even found hidden talents I never knew existed. I'm a work in progress, experiencing the positive benefits of this process on a daily basis. It is my honor and my pleasure to share it with you in *CHOICES*. Please enjoy your journey.

Part 1

LAYING THE GROUNDWORK

Chapter One: Changing the Life Pattern

Higher Selves Quote

Each of you is the only one true prophet. This simply means that it is time to begin to look inward toward the truth of your own beingness and to reach a point of becoming absolutely discerning of every single bit of information that you hear and read. For in each instance, you, as your own true prophet, must make the decision whether or not what you hear is true for you.

Begin to discern. Listen to words that are given to you. It is time to take responsibility for your own understanding and for your own information. To give someone else the burden of being the authority in your life creates for you a shadow in your own Light. Examine very carefully the shadows within your own life. Who speaks for you? Do not mindlessly seek words. Be aware. Be conscious of the words that are given to you and discern. *

* All quotes from the Higher Selves were taken from a reading for an individual, a conscious meditation group, or a Higher Self class.

Sometimes we look to others to be the masters of our destiny, to lead us to where we need to go, and sometimes we are lucky enough to find out that we are our own masters. We do not have to assume someone else's reality, ideas or beliefs just because we've heard them hundreds of times. We not only have the option but the responsibility to be true to ourselves. In so doing, we can learn to be our own best guides, supporters, and creators.

It has been said that there is my truth, your truth, and the truth. What you need to do is find *the truth* that works for you, while sifting out what doesn't feel right. No one else knows your path. No one else knows what will be important and significant to you. It is your responsibility to find your own way. No one else can do it for you.

However, finding our way is neither easy nor obvious. Many beliefs are out there, giving us bits and pieces of 'have tos' and 'better nots'. Sometimes what we find is of little help, and other times we are assisted in significant ways. What we hope to gain is greater understanding, self-forgiveness and/or to have an 'a-ha' moment that changes our lives. But while there is real help out there from a multitude of sources, it takes more than a few days or weeks to get there. Usually, there are many questions and many aspects of our lives that can be problematic. Often what is helpful in one area may not be helpful in another. Or one area improves while the others stay the same or get worse. Where is the balance?

What we are talking about is the human condition. We all have relationship issues with family members/neighbors/mates/co-workers. We all have patterns that keep recurring in life despite our efforts to change them. We experience frustrations, doubts, guilt, loneliness, isolation, fears, sadness, grief, health issues, and so much more. We all have emotional upheavals that not only have a major impact on our lives, but also often make us behave in ways in which we're not proud. And of course there can be chronic financial problems, which cut across all cultures, religions and socio-economic levels. Is there a way we can bring balance and harmony to all fronts? Is there a silver bullet? Perhaps. For some people, including myself, the Higher Self information, from the frequency level of the 5th Dimension, is just such a phenomenon. *CHOICES* will show you the path of the

Higher Selves and map it out clearly. The Higher Selves and the 5th Dimension are explained in Chapter Two, but for now, you can think of them as another resource, like a library book or an Internet site.

The Higher Selves, of course, are one source of truth. They don't ask anyone to *believe* what they say. Instead, they suggest that we each stand between belief and disbelief, allowing the information and energy to exist in the moment. They also advise that we don't take in any ideas or concepts, including theirs, as an absolute truth. Truth is ever expanding and if you lock into it today, you may shut the door to tomorrow's expansion. *Discover what truth works for you, remembering that you are your own best prophet.*

The Basis for Real Change

We have been programmed to think that change is like the drive-thru lane for fast food. If we just state what we want (more money), pay the price (simply think positive thoughts), we can pick up our food (the big check). *CHOICES* will show you that, even though change can sometimes come quickly, it is often more complicated. What happens when you go through the drive thru and the big check isn't there, or the pick-up window is closed?

In relationships, for example, if only sound bytes of communication (emails, IMS, and text messages) are a substitute for being together and getting to know one another, there will be no deep connection, no meaningful interaction, and no hope for the relationship to build and last. The same is true with our relationship to ourselves and to our lives. The drive-thru lane is best used only once in a while. If you want significant life-altering change, the quickie approach can lead to disappointment, hopelessness and feelings of failure. We all know that it takes motivation: *You have to want to change*. Where there's a will, there's a way.

Real change requires consistent inward focus. It is not about blaming your parents, your boss, your neighbor, your mate, or your genes for what's wrong in your life, nor is it about expecting someone else to fix it. It's also not about punishing or judging yourself as a loser, bad person, idiot, etc. Change is about looking within, making the choice to do the inner work, and knowing that you deserve this second chance in life. *CHOICES* introduces a lifelong process that expands your ideas, your reality, and even your consciousness. *CHOICES* can help you realize your true potential. And it is immensely doable.

The information comes from a framework outside of our normal senses. It will introduce you to ideas, perspectives and knowledge that (like most philosophies, sciences and academic subjects) include their own vocabulary. For this reason, the next chapter will present you with the concepts laid out by the Higher Selves, which come from a frequency level of the 5th Dimension. Though you may see similarity to other concepts with which you are already familiar, it is important to clarify the Higher Self Voice so that misunderstandings can be avoided. Other terms will be explained as the book progresses, and there is also an extensive Glossary at the back of the book for a quick guide.

Chapter Two: Introducing Spiritual Evolutionary Concepts

Higher Selves Quote

You unlock this door with the key of imagination. Beyond it is another dimension—a dimension of sound, a dimension of sight, a dimension of mind. You're moving into a land of both shadow and substance, of things and ideas. That's the signpost up ahead—your next stop, the Twilight Zone.

—Composite opening narration from *The Twilight Zone,* as recited by series producer, host and writer, Rod Serling.

Okay, I'm thinking most of us right now have *The Twilight Zone* theme music going through our heads. Had he known about it, perhaps Rod Serling would have used some of the upcoming information in one of his episodes. What's important here is that we go beyond our normal boundaries of imagination, opening ourselves up to the possibility of the truth from the 5th Dimension becoming part of our truth.

As discussed in the Preface, the original voice of the Higher Self information was Joan Culpepper, an extraordinarily talented woman. Over a period of about 20 years, Joan accessed information from the Higher Selves, who dwell in a higher frequency level called the 5th Dimension. To connect with the Higher Selves, Joan shifted her consciousness, raised it into this 5th Dimensional energy field, and received the information as clearly as she would hearing it in person. She called it "going into frequency" to distinguish it from channeling and psychic reading. It is this information, plus my own 25 years of experience with it, that is presented in this book. (For more information on Joan's life, please see Appendix I.)

The information provided is not scientifically proven (at least not yet) since it comes from somewhere we cannot measure with current scientific techniques. However, once you accept the premise that the information is coming from a place you can't touch, see, or hear with the normal five senses, you will find it to be logical, consistent, practical and powerful. Just like you can go outside and feel whether it is hot or cold without looking at a thermostat, you can also feel or sense that 5th Dimensional information and energy is real. You are always encouraged to decide whether or not the information is valid for you. But if you dismiss it out of hand, you can lose an important opportunity to get help.

The Originating Source of All That Is

The information from the 5th Dimension includes the assertion that there is a Higher Power, a Divine Source of energy, which is available to all. It is a neutral, balanced energy that is the Source of All There Is. However, this does not make this information/ philosophy a religion. There is no worship, no guru/priest/rabbi, no Bible, Torah or Koran, and no temple, church or other house of worship. The acknowledgment of the Divine, however, does add a spiritual element to the information and may turn some away. Please realize the information is highly practical and usable whether you believe in the Divine or not. Belief has never been one of the requirements to receive benefit.

During a Higher Self session led by Joan Culpepper, the Higher Selves directed her to use the term *Originating Source of All That Is*, or simply *Originating Source* for short, instead of the more common words of God, Jehovah, Allah, Ultimate Source, etc.

Joan had used the term Ultimate Source for years, and the Higher Selves explained that this new term presented no bias toward any one religion or belief system. They also explained that the term "Originating Source" does not carry with it any connotations—good, bad or indifferent. Most people have their own idea of the Divine Energy source, such as God "the father," a God that sits on a throne, God as judge, God as male or God as female. Originating Source is meant to encompass all words for God and is free of any attached associations. Using this neutral term allows us to receive the expanded information and energy without the limitations of preconceptions.

The Pure Soul Essence

We have often heard that God is all around us and within each of us, and that we are all connected to one another. If you're like me, you might take this statement for granted, even though you can't truly grasp the concept. Yet, the Higher Selves explain that this is so. Envision the Originating Source as a giant ball of light and with billions and billions of threads of Light extending outward. At the end of each thread is a tiny brilliant ball of Light housed within each soul in the Universe, from the smallest grain of sand to the most highly evolved being. Therefore, as this symbolic picture illustrates, within each of us is a spark of Light that is a vital part of the Originating Source. This Light, a symbol of our *Pure Soul Essence*, holds within it our highest, most pure, most perfect point of power that connects us to the Totality of All That Exists and to every other soul.

The Higher Selves often gave us symbols when describing complicated ideas. Having a mental picture can help us grasp a complicated or new concept. It is not the symbol, however, that carries the energy. When you focus on the symbol, whether through thought, visualization or imagination, that focus unlocks a very real energy. A symbol then is a focal point used to call forth the energy stream it represents.

For the Pure Soul Essence, the Higher Selves often use the symbol of Light, as well as another symbol. This second symbol, more of a picture for us to focus on, is that of two four-sided pyramids attached at the base, forming a diamond, with rainbow-colored streams of energy emanating from its various facets. Each color is symbolic of an aspect of the Originating Source. To become one with your Pure Soul Essence, you can either visualize yourself standing inside of this diamond, imagining that you are encompassed by the Light or just thinking that you are completely one with it. All methods will be equally effective since it is the same powerful energy stream that is being accessed, no matter which approach you use.

CHOICES will show you how to use this Pure Soul Essence Light to help yourself and draw from its highest source of perfected power. On a moment-to-moment basis our Pure Soul Essence carries all that the Originating Source *was, is and is becoming*—the totality of Its wisdom, knowledge, energy and experience. By consciously focusing on it, we can access the Divine Energies and draw them to us. It is a declaration from within saying, “I lay claim to my power,” the power we all carry at the Pure Soul Essence level. This is not a power that we can manipulate or misuse in any way because it comes from Divine Will. So when you are one with your Pure Soul Essence, you will be drawing from the Totality of Originating Source. Its energy won’t be marred or distorted by any emotional issues or negative thoughts you may carry in the moment. In other words, it is our way to bypass the foibles of the human condition and to have access to All That Is in the Highest Ideal.

The 5th Dimension Explained

Despite what any of us may believe, there is more to the Universe than what has been described by any past or present religious or metaphysical beliefs. Evolution doesn't go from animal to man and then from man back to God. In order to return to the Originating Source, a soul's journey is a long and complex one, taking billions and billions of years. At the human level we are only just halfway there. So what is the 5th Dimension? Where does it fit into this immense journey?

The 5th Dimension is the 5th Level of Evolutionary Awareness. Envisioning the steps on a ladder, the first step, or 1st Dimension, is the Mineral Kingdom—the planet. The next step, or 2nd Dimension, is the Plant Kingdom—all the flowers, trees, grasses, seaweed, algae, etc., that make up the flora around the world. The next step, the 3rd Dimension, is the Animal Kingdom—all the insects, fish, birds, mammals and reptiles that share the planet with us. The next step, the 4th Dimension, is the Human Kingdom, containing all the people on the planet, regardless of race, stature, location, religion or socio-economic level. The fifth step, then, is the *5th Dimension*, which houses souls who have *graduated* from human to the next level of existence.

The 5th Dimension is where all human souls are headed. It is the next stop for us in a long journey. Beyond the 5th Dimension are even two more Dimensions, the 6th and 7th, through which all souls evolve before returning to the Originating Source, from which all souls came.

It's easy to understand evolution up to the existence of Homo Sapiens—people—because it has already happened on Earth. We have seen much evidence of primitive and now-extinct plants (giant ferns the size of houses), animals (dinosaurs), and even humans (Neanderthals) that have lived over eons of time on this planet. If we paid attention in biology class, we could see how living beings developed and changed as millions of years went by. It may be a challenge, however, to get behind the idea that evolution continues on past human beings because it has not yet happened on this planet. However, as a concept, there is nothing that says evolving past human could not happen. In fact, it is exciting to think of humans moving forward to become more than what we are now.

According to the Higher Selves, there have been humans before us on millions of other planets who have completed the human phase of existence and have evolved into the 5th Dimension and beyond. Graduating from human to 5th Dimensional, however, does not involve the physical body going through changes over the millennium to become a new type of species. Instead, it involves a shift in consciousness, bringing an individual to the point where he or she understands that physical death is no longer an option—one's body will move into the 5th Dimension, along with the soul.

Graduating into the 5th Dimension is highly complex, with all of humanity moving toward this goal, and each soul moving at its own pace as it takes its own route. It involves millions of lifetimes because the process of reaching this level of consciousness is a long one. Beings that have evolved to the 5th Dimension continue up the evolutionary ladder but never again experience the process of physical death.

To further clarify, the 5th Dimension is not the same thing as Heaven. Heaven houses souls that have left the physical body and are therefore still a part of the Human Kingdom Universe. Once souls graduate to the 5th Dimension, their bodies no longer die. Therefore, they have no need to go to the Heaven between each physical life as human souls do.

Even though we can't touch Heaven, we know of its existence from many sources (other than the Higher Selves). We have read about or maybe even know of someone who remembers the experience of temporarily dying and then returning to life. The phenomenon of ghosts is well documented by ghost trackers and parapsychology researchers. There are also many people here on Earth who can communicate with the dead, and some of us have even experienced a connection with a loved one who has passed on. We know there is a Heaven, even though we may not understand exactly where it is, how it works, or why it is there.

All the evolutionary Dimensions—the Mineral, Plant, Animal, Human, 5th, 6th, and 7th—coexist. We can see that we live together on the planet with the three lower dimensions, but the other three—5th, 6th, and 7th—run at such a high evolutionary rate of speed that we don't see them. It is as if they are invisible, simplistically speaking. The Originating Source, therefore, does not 'live' in the Human Kingdom Heavens. It is the capstone of all evolution and encompasses the Totality of All There Is.

Because Heaven is a concept we have heard about since childhood, we accept at some level that it exists, even though we can't see, touch or hear it. As the concept of the 5th Dimension is a new one for most of you, it may take time to accept. Yet I feel confident that as you read *CHOICES*, you will learn about and benefit from the 5th Dimensional information. In time, your comfort level with this new idea will expand. What is important now is that the information from this source gives us powerful tools to help us change our lives. (For more information on the 5th Dimension and the evolution of a soul, stay tuned for my next book on the Universe.)

Higher Selves Introduction

The connection we have to this information, energy, and help from the 5th Dimension is the *Higher Selves.* The term Higher Selves is not an original one, and others may define it differently. As defined here, the Higher Selves are conscious thought projections from those in the 5th Dimension who work with and for us. Because direct contact with the very intense 5th Dimensional frequency could be harmful, the projection is de-intensified, brought down to a frequency level that humans can handle. These thought projections are not from aliens, like you would see in *The Twilight Zone* or any sci-fi movie. They are from souls, once fully human, who have now graduated into the 5th Dimension. Since their bodies are still there, they project their consciousness to wherever it is needed. We can tune into this consciousness level, work with the Higher Selves, and learn from them. As part of their own destiny pattern, these 5th Dimensionals assist the evolutionary process aiding all the lower kingdoms, including Human.

Why do we work with the Higher Selves instead of the Originating Source? We actually always work with both. However, the Higher Selves can be likened to a teaching assistant (TA) for a University Professor. TAs often help students understand the material in the class when the professor is so brilliant, he doesn't know how to bring the explanations down to a simpler level. Similarly, the Higher Selves help us understand our evolutionary goals, where we are going, why and even how. They are in place to help us get there, encouraging each of us over and over to focus within, to find our own answers, our own path and to fully connect with our Pure Soul Essence, the source and key to becoming more than we are now.

When we ask them, the Higher Selves provide productive, practical and powerful guidance. And if we develop a relationship and partnership with our *own* Higher Selves (everyone has access to Higher Selves who specifically work with and for *them*), we benefit greatly from the tools and techniques they offer. They help take us out of our limited belief systems and open up a world of new options and new perceptions. And as we move forward, we become more and more aware that we are our own source of information and personal power. The prison walls behind which we keep ourselves begin to fall away and the doors unlock. It is a process of true self-discovery, dissolving the old misunderstandings and misconceptions that have kept us from creating and celebrating a balanced and fulfilled life.

Anyone can call on their Higher Selves without knowing who they are. They know who we are. We don't have to see them, hear them or feel them, even though there are many who can or will develop that ability. They are there just when we think about them. However, the Higher Selves cannot trespass our free will (to be discussed in the next chapter); they have to be asked to assist us.

For those of you who are aware of and use information from master teachers or spirit guides, please understand that they are not the same as Higher Selves. While many of these teachers and guides carry important information, they are in the Human Kingdom Heavens, humans who are between lives. The master teachers train for many centuries to help we humans who are incarnate in our physical bodies. It is the 5th Dimensionals who train these master teachers. Therefore, if you want the Higher Selves to be your informational source, it is important to ask for them rather than other teachers. Meanwhile, the Higher Selves cannot and will not push aside any other helpers you have called in, since it would be trespassing your free will. (When it comes to spirit guides, psychics, channelers, master teachers, mediums and disincarnate humans, there is much more to cover. It is not within the scope of this book to do so. This topic will be covered extensively in the next book on the Universe.)

It is also important to understand that the Higher Selves are not your saviors. This is not about giving yourself over to their will or putting your fate in their hands in order to make it into Heaven or to be spiritual. While we look to the Higher Selves for help, their prime focus is to help us help ourselves. The information that you receive from them could be looked upon as yet another resource like any other you may use. They are neither higher beings that need to be worshipped nor the answer to your prayers. Instead, the Higher Selves are here to help you see that you have the answer to your own prayers, that you carry the Divine within yourself, and that you can create just the life for yourself that you have always wanted while on your evolutionary journey.

Individual Higher Self Experiences

The process of communicating with the Higher Selves is different than a medium giving voice to a deceased human. It is a process of reaching into a higher-frequency energy stream of consciousness and *hearing* the information projected there from the Higher Selves. As we each build a connection to our Higher Selves, we each will experience the process in different ways. Most people won't receive it in exactly the same way as Joan Culpepper did, word-for-word, as if reading from a document. I still use the information she gave us in her classes so many years ago because it is so clear, concise, and on tape. It was always meant to be a springboard for us all to move out on our own.

There are many ways people hear the Higher Selves. For example, one man I know hears them through writing in a journal. He begins with a thought, a problem, or an issue and ends with the insight, the answer, or a step toward resolution. Another senses it through the feeling state, feeling the solutions and the emotional impact of the information. Some see it in symbols and others in streams of color. For me, I receive it through my logical intuition. When I call the Higher Selves in, thoughts come to me as if I'm giving myself the information. I become much smarter, as insights and answers suddenly flow into my mind.

Engaging in Your Higher Self Connection

How do you begin to develop your own connection with the Higher Selves? You can ask them a question that you may have. Or you can ask for their help with a problem or tough situation. You may not hear an answer, but it doesn't mean that it didn't come to you. Notice your ideas over the next day/s. Maybe you will think about an issue in a new way or see a solution you never saw before.

One way of hearing the Higher Selves is to imagine what they would say. In the conscious meditation class, they recommended that we imagine their answers if we didn't hear them directly, since they can communicate with us through our imagination. I, for one (as I spoke about in the Preface), used the imagination process for a very long time before the information began coming through more directly. Imagining can be the beginning of your partnership. You can amalgamate any time with the Higher Selves (please see Chapter Seven) to have a dialog with them, and the more you do it, the more you will feel the connection and hear their response.

Even if you have never done it before, keeping a journal to write down what you have asked the Higher Selves and the insights or ideas that have come to you is very helpful. You can track your progress this way. You might think you'll never forget your experiences/answers, but it happens. I have many journals, and when I reread them, I am often amazed by how far I've come! They are also helping me write this book—something completely unforeseen.

So what does all of this have to do with this self-help book? It's important because the 5th Dimensional Higher Self information is the resource used in *CHOICES*. The Higher Selves provide tools for us to use, as well as a level of protection that aid us in this work. These souls, having made it beyond what we know and into other Dimensions, are there to help us with our own evolutionary process. Therefore, despite being far from our reality, this frequency level carries much practical information—an immensely expanded viewpoint of life, free of judgment and prejudice—as well as powerful energy that everyone here at the human level can tap into and use.

Chapter Three: Choices

Higher Selves Quote

It is important, as you all know, for each soul to take responsibility for his/her own life. This does not mean that as a group of individuals you cannot assist each other or help each other. What it does mean is that each individual needs to fully understand that the life he/she lives is his/her responsibility and not to lay that responsibility onto other people ("I will be happy if you do this for me"), or to the higher realms ("You do this for me then I will do this for you"), or to accept whatever is going on in your life as some 'karmic influence' (I am tied to my fate in life so there is no choice) or to lay it all on God with the idea that this is just a test.

Free Will Kingdom

Humans live in the Free Will Kingdom. The three lower Kingdoms (Mineral, Plant, and Animal) live with instinctive will. From the 5th Dimension up, souls live with Spiritual Will. Clearly, being on the human level provides us with unique and potentially difficult decisions. We are making the choices for ourselves, freely willing our present and our future. With this free will comes not only the enjoyment of our freedom and its possibilities but also responsibility for our lives and all our choices.

What this means is that all things that happen to you, for you, with you or against you are truly your choices. No experience you have, good, bad or indifferent, can happen to you against your will or without your agreeing to it. In fact, you cannot be hurt, abandoned, loved or lucky without your permission. There is no trespassing in the Free Will Kingdom. At the soul level, we agree to all we experience.

"What are you talking about?" I can hear many of you saying to that statement, followed by, "Are you nuts? I didn't ask for permission to break my leg/lose my money/have my house burn down/get dumped by my girlfriend/get this disease, etc." And I completely understand that reaction. *CHOICES* will explain how and why we choose these problems. With knowledge comes power, which enables us to take responsibility for our life experience. Responsibility for ourselves can bring us to places we never dreamed we could get to and out of places in which we thought we were doomed to stay.

Let's look at *choice* and what that means. Operating here is choice on two levels, conscious choice and unconscious choice.

Conscious Choice

Consciously making choices is only part of the picture and is perhaps the part that is easiest to understand and for which to accept responsibility. Choices with immediate and direct consequences are clearest. For example, if you jump off a roof of a two-story building, it is easy to see how that choice can cause you to break your leg/arm/head. Most people would accept responsibility for the consequence of that action. And the next time you were on the roof, you would most likely use a ladder to get down.

Indirect consequences can be more difficult to see but still may be easy for which to accept responsibility. For example, if we weren't paying good attention to how we spent our money, we would understand if we found ourselves short of funds. Or if we choose to eat poorly and not exercise, we could see how those choices contributed to a weight problem. Or, if we chose boyfriends or girlfriends who are more into their career, sports, friends, mother, father or exes than us, we could understand why we were left out/abandoned/second fiddle.

There can also be choices that give us both direct and indirect consequences. For example, let's say you practice the piano for years. Hopefully, a direct consequence would be that you learn to play the piano well. However, an indirect consequence could be a growing sense of competence, self-confidence, and self-esteem. This is easily understood.

What is more problematic for us is when we pay conscious attention to something and the outcome turns out to be unexpectedly problematic. Who here has not experienced that one? You really take time to get to know someone in a love relationship before committing and he/she seems to be completely on the same page as you about wanting kids. Then you get married, and your mate decides he/she will never be ready for children. Or how about that job you worked so hard at for years, only to be replaced by your boss's nephew as soon as he graduated from college. Clearly, all the conscious decisions and actions seemed to have you on the right track when suddenly you are out in left field.

Unconscious Choices

What we are left with then are the many things in our lives that don't seem to have anything to do with our conscious choices. You work in a factory for 20 years and it burns down one night, leaving you jobless. You buy a new computer, set it up with a surge protector, virus protector, all the latest software, and one night an extreme downpour causes a massive leak in the window air conditioner. All the equipment gets flooded and destroyed. Or simply, you are stopped at a stoplight and a car plows into you from behind. How can we possibly be responsible for these acts of nature and man when they have nothing to do with our conscious choices?

If we aren't consciously deciding everything for ourselves, there is clearly something else at work in our lives. This would be our *unconscious.* This may sound a bit like psychotherapy, but the word *unconscious,* as defined by the Higher Selves, has a specific meaning not touched on by Freud or other doctors. In *CHOICES*, the unconscious relates to the fields of etheric energy (what the Higher Selves call "envelopes") that surround the physical body of every person throughout their evolutionary sojourn. The *envelopes* of energy that are discussed in this book are the *Thought Form Body,* the *Habit Body,* the *Emotional Body*, and the *Creative Body*, They may sound a little bizarre, but in fact they are easy to understand. Let's find out what they are and how they work so that we can move on to the process of how to change our lives.

Chapter Four: How the Unconscious Works—Understanding our Etheric Bodies

Higher Selves Quote

> *The Thought Form Body is an invisible body that contains realities that have been created through every thought generated by any individual at any point in time. Within this envelope [energy field] dwells many different 'yous.' There is the 'you,' for example, who lives in this altered reality as an actual energy identity who is poor, who has no money. This altered reality has been created by you based on every thought you've projected dealing with a state of financial lack.*

This altered reality that is the 'you' in a state of financial lack actually seeks to reinforce and empower itself, the altered reality that it has become. This then, quite outside of your conscious thought process, allows that altered reality to continue to grow and manifest its power and its authority over you in the physical form in the physical reality.

Imagine what it would be like to hold on to every thought you have ever had from the first moment you were born. Imagine that each thought was actual energy that did not disappear but hung out in some energy field surrounding you. And imagine that this thought energy had some magnetic qualities so that every type of thought you'd had over the years drew all other similar thoughts to it, like magnets with the same polarity. Then imagine that all these thoughts, or *energy identities,* have created actual *altered realities* in the space around you. And as you grew up, these energy identities, and the altered realities they created, became larger and larger with each thought.

To illustrate the different concepts throughout the book, I will offer many examples in order to make them easier to understand. To do that, it will be necessary in the early stages to oversimplify somewhat. However, as each chapter unfolds, revealing additional information, more complexity is woven into the picture. By the end of the book you will see the whole of how our lives work, how each individual can take the reins of his/her life and how to achieve true change. In looking back, however, you will notice how the picture had to be broken out into various pieces before it could then become whole. Let's begin with an example of how thoughts create energy identities and how these, in turn, create altered realities.

Perhaps you're someone who has focused on your weight throughout your life. Maybe as a small child you went through a chubby stage, and sometimes people around you would suggest that you refrain from a second helping. At first you paid it no mind, but then your consciousness took it in. You began to think that you were bigger than your cousins and friends the same age. You started thinking thoughts of needing to eat less candy and desserts. You found yourself rating how some friends or family members looked based on their weight. The issue built slowly for you as you went through being teased in school.

As an adult, you've struggled with your weight, trying diet after diet with limited success. And all this time, you've been harboring thoughts about being overweight. These similar thoughts are magnetically attracted to each other, building thought forms such as "I'm too fat," "I eat too much," "I'm a failure at losing weight," and/or "I'm unlovable because I'm fat." All these thought forms tirelessly develop an altered reality of your struggling with your weight.

Thought Form Body

Thoughts of every type have created thought forms in each of us. They come in all sizes—some tiny and some huge, with many in between, depending on the degree of thought put into them. As the Higher Selves stated in the above quote, the invisible envelope (energy field) around us, the place where these positive and negative energy identities call home, is the *Thought Form Body*. It isn't actually a physical body but is instead held in an etheric energy field everyone carries with them. It contains all the thoughts of joy, fear, love, hate, hurt, illness, wealth, poverty, and ideas of the self, others, relationships, work, play, and on and on. All thoughts are held here, magnetically attracting similar thoughts from many sources, thereby building and strengthening all of our thought forms. They create all the altered realities that live with us in our Thought Form Body.

Suspending disbelief for a minute, let's take this a few steps further by looking at how our mind works. Do we tend to think more positively or negatively as we go throughout our day? Most of you know the answer to this already.

For example, if we wake up feeling good, having had a good night's sleep, we might think, "Oh, I feel great today! I have so much energy; I'm sure this will be a good day." And then we go on our way and may never think of it again. Despite feeling really good, we actually tend to spend little time thinking about it. Feeling good helps us focus on the things we have to accomplish that day, resulting in thoughts geared toward those activities other than the state of feeling good.

But what happens if we sleep poorly and wake up with a backache, headache, or stiff neck? Don't we often express a litany of complaints about it to friends or co-workers? And if a repairman or deliveryman comes by and politely asks, "How are you," what do we say? If we feel good, we most likely just say, "Fine, and you?" But if our neck still hurts, we say, "Well, since you asked, I am having a bad day, starting with…"

The tendency to dwell on the negative outweighs our tendency to think positively, and every day we do so we strengthen those misery magnets. This means that when we look at the balance or the ratio of negative energy identities to positive ones, the scale weighs heavily on the negative side. This serves none of us well.

Drive to Manifestation

Thought forms are soulless and mindless. They lack consciousness. However, they carry the power of magnetic attraction. This magnetic energy is working 24/7. In fact, it does not just attract our own thoughts but all similar thoughts from many sources, including other people. This is not a conscious act any more than an actual magnet consciously attracts. What is the result of all this attraction?

The result of magnetic attraction is that the energy identities (and the altered realities they create) continue to build in strength. At the point that they're strong enough, they manifest into our physical reality. In fact, their sole purpose is to manifest. *The manifestation process from all of our energy identities is what forms our outer expression or, in other words, our lives.*

For example, if it is cold and rainy outside, we may think throughout the day that we have to keep warm and dry so we don't get sick. We see ads on TV about various cold remedies, which remind us to check what we have on hand just in case. We remember the time last year when we got the worst cold ever and had to miss work. Flu season is here and we plan to get a flu shot. We believe that all schools are breeding grounds for illnesses and have no patience for parents who send their children to school with a cold. We also believe that we are susceptible to every germ with which we come in contact. In this way, we are empowering our illness thought form (one that we already have) over and over again. And what do you know? Despite all our efforts to prevent it, we come down with a massive cold two weeks later and blame it on the time we spent helping out at our daughter's pre-school.

In fact, getting sick was a result of the altered reality of illness gaining enough strength to manifest itself in our physical reality as a cold. It attracted the opportunity when you were asked to volunteer to read to your child's pre-school class. This then triggered and empowered your beliefs (based on your thoughts) that you were now exposed to the germs that you were convinced would make you sick. And they did.

Isn't it just that colds are contagious? No. If that were the case, every teacher, parent, and student who came in contact with children would get sick. Each individual responds to each situation based on what thought forms he/she is creating for him/herself. That is why some children/teachers have perfect attendance and others are chronically sick or somewhere in between. Of course, this process is more complex than I have presented. But the basic principles are the same.

Other examples are: If you have a large victim thought form, it will magnetically attract conditions that will make you a victim once more. If you have a failure pattern, the thought forms will bring in situations that will again result in failure. If you bring in mates that make you crazy with their infidelity, the thought forms may keep you in a cycle of betrayal. The process of manifestation will be explained more fully in Chapter Six, but our thought forms are the primary source for the patterns we have in our lives.

Habit Body

In addition to the Thought Form Body, we also carry a *Habit Body*. The Habit Body is another invisible envelope of energy (field) surrounding us that contains imprints of every thought and every action. Thoughts create energy identities and habit imprints simultaneously. And as the imprints of similar thoughts get deeper and deeper, they become our most ingrained habits. As we smoke / worry / procrastinate / and so on, the imprints / ruts are reinforced again. In other words, the depth of a habit imprint in the Habit Body is relative to how often we have thought the thought and/or acted—the deeper the rut, the more automatic and intense the habit. There are no energy identities in the Habit Body, but the habit imprints empower the thoughts and vice versa.

Have you ever noticed that you wake up five mornings out of seven at the exact same time? Or that you get a cup of coffee without thinking before you start any project? Or that you put on your left shoe before your right one every morning? These are simple, repetitive habits that are easy to see and are relatively harmless in the scheme of things. Of course, we all have deeper and more complicated ones, so it is very important that we pay attention to all our habits. These habit imprints work with Thought Forms to reinforce our patterns. These two working together are in part what makes it so difficult to change things about ourselves with which we are unhappy. The more ingrained a habit, the more we act on it and think about it. The thought form gains power and then manifests again – and then again.

One of my habits for over ten years was to sleep only three or four hours a night. Once I woke up, I could not fall back to sleep, resulting in chronic exhaustion. Fortunately, by doing the exercises that the Higher Selves taught us, I was successful at changing this pattern, and those sleepless years are now a distant memory. Now I sleep at least five to six hours a night with few exceptions. I still wake up many nights, but the difference is I go back to sleep. Of course, five or six hours are not enough. Fortunately, I have continued to improve, sleeping seven plus hours a night at least three times every week. Habits can be changed, and you can do it too.

The Overall Picture

Remember that we live as humans in a Free Will Kingdom, that we choose how our lives unfold. If something happens that changes our thought patterns for a day or week, we will empower different energy identities and habit imprints and will, therefore, manifest differently than we did in prior weeks.

One example many can relate to is the unexpected death of a young friend or family member. The new vulnerability we now feel may make us realize that we have been complacent about life. As a result, we decide to focus more on preventing illness by eating healthy food and exercising. We also become more open to telling our family every day how much we love them and perhaps resolve to work harder to be a better person so that there are no regrets if we die young. Were we thinking this way before? No, but we are now. So our energy identities and habit imprints are changing as a reflection of the changes in our thought patterns.

What is more significant, however, is *how often we are determined to change only to find our old habits return.* How many of us with great intentions find ourselves back in the same place within days/weeks/months? How many times have we had to use the same New Year's resolution because we didn't accomplish it this year or the prior years? Why are there so many new diets on the market, multiple no-smoking aids, a myriad of solutions for depression, insomnia, etc? Why are there so many self-help books? For all our grand efforts and deep desires to change, we predictably find ourselves back in the same place, having made little lasting forward movement. This does not feel good. There are reasons why change is so hard, and this is why I wrote *CHOICES*. We need help to make the changes. There is much more to it than thinking positive thoughts. Let's take a look at the Law of Attraction.

The Law of Attraction Clarified

Higher Selves Quote

> *Thought forms are what carry the impact of what you will outwardly manifest. This is not a process that will be reached through affirmations or through consciously speaking words. For the process of thought forms is one that goes very, very deep. Thought forms are carried from lifetime to lifetime so that the buildup of these 'altered realities' is very intense and very powerful.*

What exactly is the Law of Attraction? It seems to be the basis of many metaphysical self-help books (including *The Secret*) and even has its place in some religious teachings. Simply stated, it posits that thoughts are energy and are magnetic in nature. They attract to you situations and people that match your predominant thoughts, whether conscious or unconscious. The bottom line, therefore, is like attracts like. The more positively you think, the more positive your life will be. Every individual is responsible for what they bring into their lives. Is there more to it than this? Yes.

If you have understood the information in *CHOICES* up to now, there is a good chance you see that the Thought Form Body information seems similar to the Law of Attraction. Both involve magnetic attraction that brings situations, conditions and people into our lives based on our thoughts. However, you may also be beginning to see that there needs to be more than positive thought to create real change in your life. Of course, there are people who have changed their thoughts from the negative to positive, who have brought more good into their lives than before. But what does it mean for those of us who haven't found success by thinking positively, yet have worked as hard or harder than others who do? What about those who achieved results but didn't recognize that what they got was either the exact right result (even if unexpected) or that it was only the first step in a process that would lead them to the final goal? What about the patterns that keep recurring in life despite the efforts to change them? Or the emotional upheavals that make us behave in ways we're not proud of?

What has been missing in the prior teachings on the Law of Attraction is the fact that it has not been fully understood. The Higher Selves didn't change the Law. They explain how it works. And there are two misconceptions that need to be cleared up. One, *a positive thought does not negate or replace a negative thought.* It only empowers the positive energy identities while the negative ones remain to magnetically attract negative situations, conditions and people into our lives. Because we harbor so much more of the negative, the positives we empower through our thoughts are still extremely weak compared to the powerful negatives. In Part II, *CHOICES* will describe a more efficient and powerful way to empower your positive thought forms, growing them to where they are increased 1000-fold.

The section misconception is that even if you never think a negative thought ever again, it doesn't mean that the negative energy identities go away. Once created, the thought energy exists forever. Leaving those negative altered realities in place is what makes it so difficult for us to change. Whether negative or positive, the energy remains in place in our etheric bodies as thought forms and habit imprints. When these are positive, we can rejoice. When they are negative, we are concerned with what we do about them. What we must do is to neutralize the negative energies to render them harmless and incapable of magnetically attracting anything that could hurt us. Neutralizing the negatives and using that energy to empower our Light is the key to change and is fully explained in Part II. Again, the Higher Selves didn't change the Law of Attraction but added details about how it functions. *CHOICES* will show you how you can properly utilize it to your advantage.

The Shift from Victim to Taking Charge

Once we accept that we are living in a Free Will Kingdom, and that we are making both conscious and unconscious choices that create our experiences, we can find our way to take responsibility for what happens to us. So the shift goes from blaming someone, something or some event for our problem/s to looking at ourselves and asking, "Why did I bring this into my life?" "How can I change this reality?" Or "How can I prevent it from happening again?"

There is no judgment here. We are not all screw-ups who just can't get it right. Instead, we acknowledge that we are all experiencing the human condition. Everyone has challenges to face, joys to experience, moments of wonder and moments of despair. What will be explained is the way to be actively involved in how your life unfolds. There is no magic pill to take and presto…you have changed. If it took years and lifetimes to develop our patterns, undoing these patterns won't be instantaneous. However, with consistent effort, we can change our patterns, find what was hidden and untapped, and definitely improve our lives significantly.

In a year from now we will all be one year older. We can still be in the same place, coping with the same issues. Or we can use the simple Higher Self techniques and make this year and every year a witness to us becoming much more of what we want to be. We understand our conscious choices. And now we understand how our own thought forms and habit imprints, through the process of magnetic attraction, work with our conscious choices to create the outer expression we call our lives. Someone else isn't creating our lives. It isn't Mother Nature, your jerky boss, or a vindictive god picking on you. We are busy making and playing out our patterns consciously and unconsciously, then, taking what life gives us and handling it as best we can. Now is the time to be in charge, and we *can* be. We are not doomed. We are not stuck. We are not powerless.

Chapter Five: How the Emotions Fit in

Higher Selves Quote

> *Each of the circumstances brought into play through the Thought Form and Habit Bodies creates an experience in your life that you respond to emotionally, and it is this emotional response that actually is held within your Emotional Body. The stockpile of all of your similar emotional responses becomes your emotional blueprint.*

Intense grief over the loss of a loved one and inconsolable despair when a love relationship goes wrong are examples of negative emotions all of us have felt to some degree. How about great joy at seeing our child beat a life-threatening illness, pure bliss from the throes of first love, or the deep satisfaction of a difficult job well done? These are obviously positive emotions. Emotional responses to events, experiences, and/or actions reflect the polarity present in the Human Kingdom, where emotions are seen and experienced, for the most part, as positive or negative. There is love and hate, happy and sad, satisfied and unsatisfied, with all the ranges in between. It is clear that emotions play an important role in life from any perspective, so let's take a closer look at them.

Emotional Blueprints

I think all of us have experienced the drama of emotional swings. After college I called the next nine years "my terrible twenties." It was a time of such great emotional upheaval for me: despair, anxiety and feelings of failure, etc. Sure, there were good times too …but those were overwhelmed by the bad.

I wasn't a complete drama queen but suffered personally more times than not. I'm sure in some way all of you can relate—bad relationships, career problems, not meeting the expectations of others, feelings of despair, isolation and failure while trying to pretend otherwise. The twenties became my thirties. I was unhappy that my erratic emotions dominated my life, and I still didn't have a solution for what to do about them.

In my mid-thirties help arrived in Joan's Wednesday-night group when the Higher Selves explained emotions. I was a rapt student. Similar to the Thought Form and Habit Bodies, they explained there was another invisible envelope of energy (energy field) surrounding our physical body called the *Emotional Body*. This body contained the emotional *responses* to every experience that each of us has had throughout his/her life. They went on to explain, however, that an experience is actually a neutral event not tied to any specific emotion. So how is it that we associate emotions with most experiences and how is this significant?

When we first associate an emotion with an experience and then target (blame) that person or event as the cause of that emotion, we have attached that emotion to the experience. By doing so, the experience is no longer a neutral event for us. It includes the emotional response. It is these attached emotional responses that are held in the Emotional Body.

Let's look at the example of the event where one sees a snake. This is a neutral event. If seeing a snake had an emotion attached to it, then everyone would react to it in the same way. But they do not. If someone sees a snake for the very first time, crawling across a road, that person could have a large range of emotional responses, from interest to indifference, anxiety to calm, or fascination to repugnance, based on a variety of factors. Let's say this person has heard tales about snakes being sinister animals. Then his/her first sight of the snake may make him/her afraid. Fear becomes that person's emotional response to this experience. He/she targets (blames) the snake as the cause of his/her feeling afraid (here is a snake and I am afraid of it), and there is now a fear response attached to the experience of seeing a snake. This event is no longer neutral for that person.

When he/she sees another snake, there is already an emotional response attached to the similar experience, so fear is triggered once again. As this repeated triggering of fear continues, it adds more and more power to the already-attached emotion/s. Picture a sphere that symbolically represents an experience in its neutral form, one with no emotion attached. When someone attaches an emotional response to that experience, it's as if the person has *Velcroed* the emotional response to the sphere (the experience). And each time a similar experience occurs, the emotional response is triggered because it is already attached. As the fear response recurs, it is once again attached to the experience (the sphere), adding more intensity to the emotional response each time. So (using the snake example) seeing a snake a second, third or more times would generate fear automatically, literally giving one little choice to respond differently, even if the snake was a harmless one.

We all have many hundreds of thousands of spheres representing neutral experiences with attached (Velcroed) emotional responses. The patterns of these responses are unique, created by each individual, and are not defined by the experiences themselves. Some experiences generate little emotional response, while others a great deal, depending on each individual's patterns. The more times an experience recurs, the more intensified and rigid the response pattern becomes, getting thicker and thicker and more ingrained. These emotional-response patterns are what the Higher Selves call *emotional blueprints*.

These blueprints operate as any other blueprint. They reveal how our emotional reactions to events are going to play out. Some blueprints are fairly straightforward—see snake, become afraid. Others are more complicated, involving a range of emotions that come into play, as the experience itself becomes more complicated. For example, if your son gets into a car accident, you may feel fear—wondering if he is okay; anger—that he used the cell phone while driving; frustration—as you had cautioned him often about the phone; relief—that he is okay; determination—to get more strict about the cell phone use; anxiety—about what the damaged car may cost you. You may ask, if this is the first time my son was in a car accident, why would there be a blueprint? Because the experience is part of a larger pattern, that of your child getting into any kind of accident and harming himself. This kind of experience has happened in the past, whether it was when he fell off the swing on a playground, was hit by a baseball, or accidentally ran into the closed, sliding-glass door thinking it was open. In fact you have had this experience many times as a parent of an active son. Your response blueprint was created way before today's car accident. And this example does not even include the thousands of times you had this type of experience in other lifetimes, with other offspring.

To clarify, when something happens to us, *our emotional response has already been created in the past* (of this life and all other lives) and has only been triggered by the most-recent experience. As a result, we are actually programmed to respond emotionally in the same manner for each and every similar experience, even though it feels as if we are responding to the experience like it is our first time, or as if this response is how everyone else would naturally respond. *We become so used to the whole package that we think the experience and the emotional response are virtually one and the same.*

Rarely questioning why this is so, we embark on an emotional journey when an event occurs, often thinking we are responding to it in a unique way, when, in fact, we are going down a predetermined path. We have reacted to this type of experience the same way so often that we have unknowingly created an emotional blueprint that we blindly follow for all similar events.

Pushed Buttons

Many of us have experienced having our buttons pushed, those times when something seemingly innocent or minor occurs, and we overreact with much more intensity than the moment deserves. Most tellingly, we overreact in exactly the same way each time. Whether we are afraid when we see a snake, or angry when someone cuts us off on the freeway, we know that we will experience reactions, which we don't seem to have much control over. Generally everyone understands that these responses are automatic and not completely rational. Even the person having his/her buttons pushed knows it is an overblown response.

Picture being at a party, where there is a group of three people talking—Joe, Carrie and Terry. All three are excited and happy, and at some point Joe interrupts Carrie's story in his enthusiasm to add his two cents. Objectively, it would be a relatively minor occurrence between two good friends. Carrie doesn't even notice and just interrupts Joe right back, deftly moving inside the jumble of the moment. However, Terry, who is listening, gets really irritated, and when both Carrie and Joe are finished,

Terry speaks up and berates Joe for interrupting Carrie. Both Joe and Carrie, having not even noticed the interruption, are surprised and try to calm down Terry, who is clearly heated. As he calms down, Terry says, "I'm sorry, interruptions just push my buttons." Terry has had his emotional blueprint related to interruptions triggered, and we can see that its intensity was overblown for the current situation. Again, when our blueprints get triggered, the magnitude of the response is relative to the density of the responses from all similar prior experiences and *not from current incident.*

Let's theorize that Terry had many experiences in life of being hurt because he was interrupted. This created a powerful emotional blueprint laden with his intense negative reaction to interruptions. In fact, the blueprint is so heavy that it's even triggered when someone else is interrupted. Perhaps Terry had an overbearing and intolerant father who chronically interrupted both Terry and his mother when either of them would try to speak. If his father interrupted them and then hurled insulting and hurtful comments about what they were saying, we could see how such a negative blueprint would be created. And this does not even include the many similar experiences in his thousands of prior lifetimes.

In real life we would most likely never know what could cause such an intense emotional response to interruptions (or any emotional response to any experience), but if we did, we could understand why, as an adult, Terry had these feelings. We've all experienced overreacting to situations or even having responses to things to which others can't relate. Therefore, we acknowledge that in certain situations our pushed buttons control our emotions, giving us little choice in the matter, and as a result, *we unfortunately accept that this is just who we are.*

The Bigger Picture

Although the pushed-button analogy is helpful when understanding relatively minor things, emotional blueprints are also in charge of our emotional responses to more serious experiences, such as a loved one's death, a major financial loss, or a betrayal by a spouse. While our emotions are very real, these experiences are intrinsically neutral in nature. It's the triggering of blueprints we have attached to these experiences that will most likely play out intense emotional responses that have a significant effect on our lives. So when we feel grief over the death of a loved one, we are feeling the grief intensified by all the grief we have felt over the span of our soul's journey. We spend time and money on therapy and doctors as we cope with the effects of powerful emotions that cause ulcers, crying jags, crippling guilt, sleepless nights, anxiety attacks, and/or blaming others for our anger, frustrations, hurts and wounds, etc. In general, we often behave based on our emotional baggage—these emotional blueprints—instead of the emotions we are feeling during the *now* of an experience, which would not have any intrinsic emotional attachments.

If we didn't have our blueprints, we would still have emotions and would respond emotionally to each experience, but the emotional response would be based on the experience itself and not on the pre-programmed replays. So if someone saw a snake safely kept in a cage, there would be no fear, perhaps only interest or sadness from seeing a caged animal. Still, our blueprints are there, and until we understand how to be free of these attached emotional responses and how to properly process emotions, we will continue to be controlled by them.

Who wants to experience life events that are polluted with decades and lifetimes of emotional responses, driving us to respond in the same way for each type of experience, taking *real choice* out of our options? Just as with thoughts forms, most of this baggage is negative and acts as an anchor to hold us connected to negative experiences. The emotional drama provokes continuous thoughts about the issue/subject/person/ event, which in turn increases the magnetic power of the related thought forms and habits. Working together as part of our unconscious, the energy identities, habit imprints and emotional blueprints empower and create the patterns we find in our lives.

Unconsciously Defining Ourselves—Self Identities

In addition, it is these emotional blueprints that often create how we define our nature, such as, "I always cry at weddings," or "I can't tolerate stupidity," or "I always get angry when someone teases me." Even more significant are statements like, "I am just a moody person," or "I'm always ashamed of…" or "I'm competitive to a fault," or (what I used to say), "I'm an emotional basket case." These emotional blueprints lock us into repetitive response patterns that make us assume we are a certain kind of person. These become our self-identities—that we are heartless, reckless, overbearing, living in the past, unlucky, desperate, vulnerable, anxious, etc. What if we really could be who we wanted to be and not who we have previously programmed ourselves to be? What an idea!

Even if we somehow knew how and why our easily pushed buttons developed, it wouldn't be enough to solve the problem. We need to know how to remove theses emotional blueprints, which keep us chained to our patterns and focused on our negative thoughts. It's difficult to imagine, but an absolutely attainable goal. We have the ability to neutralize our emotional baggage, thus freeing ourselves from the stranglehold that our emotional patterns have on us. We have choice as to how we feel!

Chapter Six: The Creative Body

Higher Selves Quote

> *The Creative Body is the body that harnesses the energy and slowly begins to weave the pattern that will ultimately filter through and manifest within the physical reality. The Creative Body contains all the potential creations (manifestations) as they exist in your life at any point in time. It is that body of energy that is read by psychics who work in areas involving psychic prediction.*

We have now learned about thought forms, habit imprints, and emotional blueprints, but how do they all work together? Do they cooperate? Fight one another? Hang out watching life go by? Actually, they are consolidated in yet another large etheric envelope (field) of energy—which also surrounds the physical body—called the *Creative Body.*

The Creative Body carries the *Creative Life Force* energy, energy that is soulless and mindless but nonetheless creates from moment to moment. Using the energies of thought forms, habits and emotional blueprints we carry from this lifetime and every other lifetime, the powerful Creative Life Force weaves the patterns that will ultimately filter through and manifest into the physical realm, our lives. *In other words, it is in your Creative Body that your outward physical life is manufactured.* And to be even clearer, the Creative Life Force energy doesn't care if what it is creating is positive or negative. It doesn't care if it is something you want or don't want. It creates solely based on the strength of the thoughts, habits, and emotional blueprints you harbor at any moment in time. Whatever an individual carries is what is used to create his/her life. Let's look at an example.

The economy has just begun to go south. The unemployment rate is rising. Businesses are going belly up. Personal bankruptcy is at epidemic levels, and pundits on the economy are predicting doom and gloom. Josh, a man in his forties, is taking in this news. He is responding with the emotional blueprint of fear. In each of the prior downturns, he lost his job, so fear of losing his job becomes his programmed response. The fear intensifies and empowers his job-loss thought form and habit imprints as he worries and obsesses. Within his Creative Body—using the energies of these habits, thought forms and emotional blueprints—the Creative Life Force energy is *weaving* the loss of his current job, which will eventually manifest in his life.

But wait…let's look at other parts of the scenario. Josh also believes that he is irreplaceable. This time he thinks he has job security and, as such, has empowered this positive thought form. Inside the Creative Body, the positive also gives energy to what he manifests. This could prevent him from losing his job completely or perhaps delay a layoff.

But let's look even deeper at what else Josh carries. If he also has a powerful thought form about never being able to establish financial security in life, the positive effect of his job security thought form may not change his creation (what he manifests) much at all, except for, perhaps, a minor delay in his layoff—especially since we know that the positive energy identities are smaller than the negative ones. But what if Josh also believes that even if he is never quite financially secure, he will always have some money coming in? This may result in a 20% cut in salary or hours, but not the loss of his job.

In fact, it is so much more complicated than even this. Many other thought forms, habits and emotional blueprints factor into what Josh manifests. He could have self-esteem issues triggering his belief that he will never get ahead in life. There could also be an identity issue where he feels more connected to being a Dad than a breadwinner, feeling more successful at taking care of his kids than at his work. Is he consciously thinking about all these things? Probably not. Are we ever going to be aware of all that goes into our own creations? I sincerely doubt it, only because of how complex the weave is. And that is okay. We don't need to know (though if interested, we can develop an awareness of many of them). I gave the above example so that we have some basic understanding of how the various parts of our unconscious work to create our lives, and also to make it clear that any negative occurrence in life, such as Josh's potential job loss or salary cutback, is woven from what we would call both negative and positive thought forms. Therefore, thinking positively is not the sole answer. There is more to life's problems than what appears on the surface.

We Are Responsible for How External Events Affect Our Lives

Many of us believe that external events are out of our control and that we are not responsible for the effect they have on our lives. If Josh loses his job, he will most likely feel it was for one reason: the bad economy. He won't question his assumption. And we can all understand that because we have made those types of assumptions ourselves.

It is extremely hard to fully grasp the concept that we have any say in our lives when an external event such as a bad economy (or a natural disaster) creates major problems for so many. That we have no control or say in the results is what we have learned our whole lives. We believe that being caught in a collapsing building during an earthquake is horrible luck, or if like Josh, that our job loss was caused by the recession. However, if the bad economy is the only thing responsible for people losing their jobs, why don't we see everyone getting laid off? Why isn't there an unemployment rate of 95%? The reason is that the economic downturn triggers thought forms, habits and emotional blueprints *within each individual in its own unique way, weaving different outer realities for each.* Therefore, each person will go through a downturn (or any other major event) manifesting a unique outcome, depending on the blend and intensity of what each carries in their etheric bodies.

We know that in every recession and depression there are always people who do even better than they did in good times. There are also others who manage to break even, without moving up or down financially, and then there are those who become destitute, losing their work, home and even marriages. In reality, the population reflects the wide range of economic results because every soul is a snowflake—no two individuals are the same. What we manifest in our outer reality reflects all that we each uniquely carry in our etheric bodies.

Please understand that there is no judgment against someone who manifests severe problems in an economic downturn, or in any other time. This is not about categorizing people as failures or losers. Judgment has no bearing on what is truly happening. We all carry a huge mix of energy identities, and the person who has a hard time keeping a job may be a caring person, a talented artist, or the best Little League coach ever. How well one person does or does not do should never become an opportunity to judge or insult someone or yourself; it's only a good chance to understand that we all have patterns which originate in our unconscious and are being created in our outer reality 24/7. This understanding gives us hope that things can be different once we have the tools and techniques to modify what we are holding in our unconscious.

Now that we have the basic concepts of how things work, the next step is the *process*, taking the actions that will help us be in charge of what we create. The Creative Life Force energy may not care what type of outcomes it manufactures, but we care. We all want to manifest good in our lives instead of crises, drama, grief or suffering. Let's take the chance and go for it.

Part 2

THE SOUL / MIND DETOX

Chapter Seven: The Process Overview

Higher Selves Quote

In working with the idea of neutralizing the thought forms within your Thought Form Body and cauterizing the imprints of your Habit Body, you can bring yourself to a point in this reality where you are materially and spiritually balanced, thereby allowing yourself to manifest into this physical reality a more perfectly attuned physical life.

*****

It is the emotional blueprints that act as a web to confine and restrict emotional expression. In this processing, what you will be neutralizing is the webbing, not the emotions themselves. The emotions will be released and the restriction will be neutralized.

The question now is what to do about these thought forms, habits and emotional blueprints that are currently creating our lives in ways that we assume we can't change. Thankfully, the Higher Selves have given us a powerful exercise that everyone can do. It shifts the balance of energy identities from predominantly negative to mainly positive. This results in manifesting more of what we want in life and less of what we don't want. The exercise is like a detox that purges your soul/mind of the misunderstandings, false assumptions and erroneous conclusions built up into hardened layers over many years and lifetimes. This soul/mind detox must occur before you can begin to experience the truly magnificent life that is your birthright.

There are dozens of exercises we can use, and several will be shared in this book. However, there is one basic but essential exercise—what I like to call the *Key Exercise*. If nothing else is done on a consistent basis but this one exercise, you will absolutely be able to change your life. It is the one exercise I do almost daily, whether it is for a few minutes or more. It's explained in Chapter Ten. For now, more context and explanation are needed in order to understand fully the exercise most effectively.

There are three simple parts to the exercise and they are: the *Amalgamation*, the *Neutralization* of the negative and the *Empowering* of the positive. The following is a brief explanation of all three.

The Amalgamation

Before we start this and all other exercises, we first do what the Higher Selves call an Amalgamation. The term *Amalgamation* simply means to unite, to blend, to become one with. We use this Amalgamation process to become one with our Higher Selves energy, our own Pure Soul Essence and the Originating Source.

The reason for the Amalgamation is twofold. First, remember that we have to ask the Higher Selves and the Originating Source to help, since they cannot trespass our free will. Therefore, the Amalgamation is our way of inviting them to help with the process. Second, the energy gives us two levels of protection. The Higher Self energy moves in through and around the physical and etheric bodies (to the degree your body can handle it) to act as a filtering unit that prevents us (during the amalgamation) from magnetically attracting negative energies. Also, because there is so much that we can't see, touch, feel or completely understand, amalgamating will automatically align us with our Highest Ideal and with Divine Will. This action guarantees that the exercise we are about to perform will be done in a way that is perfect for each individual. This is the safety valve assuring us that we don't accidentally do more harm than good. If, for example, you are working to heal your knee and your hip actually needs the healing, your hip will benefit instead.

Neutralizing the Negative

The second part of the Exercise is to *neutralize* our negative thought forms, habits and emotional blueprints. Keep in mind that the Law of Magnetic Attraction holds equally true for our negative energy identities as it does for the positive ones. No matter how many positive thoughts we may have, they do not neutralize our negative thoughts. Every thought (positive or negative) is drawn to the like energy identities. All of these give power to what is created in our outer reality. *Therefore, it is essential to make the negative energy identities harmless, to put a stop to their magnetic power.* To do this, we neutralize the negative thought forms, habit imprints and emotional blueprints.

To neutralize these, we use the Pure Soul Essence Light. The neutralizing process will reduce the magnetic power of these soulless and mindless but powerful negative energy identities. The less power they carry, the less negative fuel there is to feed the Creative Life Force energy, thereby reducing the negative manifestations in our outer physical reality. Remember that we are trying to shift the balance here from weighing heavily on the negative side to weighing heavily on the positive side.

Neutralization of the negative energy identities can be viewed as a *detoxification* process. We carry so many misconceptions, fears, doubts, angry feelings and much more that have accumulated over our lifetimes. There are layers and layers of buildup (encrustments) that blind us as to who we truly are, that holds us prisoner to the misery of difficulties around us and/or prevents us from manifesting all that we deserve and wish for. The Key Exercise is a powerful tool that enables us to clear away this debris. It works like a giant vacuum that pulls in and absorbs the negative layers, which steadily uncovers the beauty and joy we all carry underneath.

Empowering the Positive

This step is essential as well. With each positive thought, the positive thought forms are growing in size and magnetic power. However, even if we focus on positive thoughts all day long, it could take several months or most likely years for such thinking to have a significant impact on our lives, because we carry a great abundance of negative thoughts from so many lifetimes. To speed this empowerment process up, the Higher Selves suggest that we also use the Pure Soul Essence Light to add massive energy to the positive thought forms. This empowering is only done on the thought forms, not on the habit imprints or emotional blueprints. For example, as the thought form of material abundance grows, it automatically creates the habit imprints. And since the goal is to neutralize our emotional blueprints so that we are free to choose how we feel for each and every experience, we do not empower any emotional blueprint—positive or negative.

Keep in mind that empowering the energy identities with our Pure Soul Essence Light will build the positive thought forms at light speed compared to thinking one positive thought at a time.

It is important to be conscious of your thoughts and to be in a positive frame of mind. However, so much of the time we can be so overwhelmed by what is going on in life that we can easily fall back into our negative thought patterns. I am here to encourage you not to despair or to feel like you are failing. You can us the Key Exercise daily and it will allow you to neutralize those negative thoughts and to empower the positive ones. As a result, you will find that a positive state of mind comes much more easily and naturally.

Chapter Eight: Other Essential Elements

Since *consciousness is power*, there are three elements explained below that need to be addressed so that the exercise will be as effective as possible. The three elements are as follows:

PAST LIVES

Higher Selves Quote

> *The soul is the minds of the past and holds at that level a Thought Form Body. In the Thought Form Body of the soul are the collected thoughts connected to that soul from all of the past lifetimes. These then feed the current mind pattern, creating and reinforcing the Thought Form Body of the current mind in the current lifetime.*

Many of you already believe that past lives have an effect on our current life. And in passing I've indicated as such in the previous chapters. Now, however, it is important to be clear. When we are born into a life, our current *mind*, we arrive with a clean Thought Form body, a clean Habit Body and a clear Emotional Response Body. However, the formation of the thought forms, habit imprints, and emotional blueprints begin almost immediately. Since an infant doesn't have conscious thought, where do they come from?

Our thoughts from the past *give birth* to the thoughts in this lifetime. When we die, the thoughts from the most recent lifetime are added on to the thoughts of all the other prior lifetimes. Then, when we are born again, we bring in all those thought forms from all of our past lives. We call these past-life energy identities, *the parents*, and they give birth to the current life thought forms, or *the children*. (This happens with the habit imprints and the emotional blueprints as well, but for simplicity, I will only describe this process with thought forms.)

Let's use the example of illness. You are a newly born infant carrying clear etheric bodies as you begin the current life. However, with you are all the thoughts of your thousands of prior lifetimes, including thoughts of all the illnesses ever experienced in those lives. The illness thought form (as do all others) immediately begins to magnetically attract to it similar energy, and by doing so, gives birth to itself in the current life. If the soul is carrying a very powerful illness thought form, it could mean that the infant gets ill very quickly, either with something simple or more serious. If it is not a powerful thought form, the infant may just experience its first cold at few months old or much later. In either case, the thought form of illness from prior lifetimes has given birth to illness in this lifetime.

What does this mean for the work that we do with the Key Exercise? Again, the process is very simple. When we work on the soul/mind detox by doing the Key Exercise explained in Chapter Ten, we include the neutralizations of both the parents and the children of all of our thought forms, imprints, and blueprints. This way, our reservoir of past-life negative thought forms (the parents) can be decreased as well, thereby, greatly reducing the probability of rebuilding the negative thought forms in this life (the children).

DIRECTLY AND INDIRECTLY RELATED THOUGHT FORMS

Higher Selves Quote

Within the Thought Form Body there is an altered reality (created by the energy identities) that runs headlong out of breath, out of time consistently. This then manifests outward into your own reality. In your Thought Form Body there is also an altered reality that is very, very tired, an altered reality that is very, very lazy, and an altered reality that has many reasons for going off in nine different directions at once. All of these particular realities related to time cooperate with each other very. There are many altered realities within the Thought Form Body that can be neutralized, which will immediately enable you to discipline your time.

Whether your issues are time management, relationships, financial lack, or Josh's job-loss pattern, there are many thought forms that work together to create a pattern. The manifestation of our outer reality is the result of a complex and convoluted weaving of our energies. Some of the energy identities are directly involved and may be easy to identify. Others would be indirectly involved and may not be remotely possible to identify.

Does it help to just work on one or two of the direct thought forms since we may not know exactly what the other indirect thought forms actively involved are? Yes, of course. Any work to neutralize thought forms is helpful. There is also a way to work on the ones of which we are not aware. As you have already learned, what seems complicated is often quite simple.

It is extremely empowering to include all the thought forms involved with the pattern we wish to neutralize, *both direct and indirect*. Just by adding this concept to the Key Exercise, all the energy identities will be included as we do the work, whether we know what they are or not.

CAUSES AND RIPPLE EFFECTS

Higher Selves Quote

> *It is unnecessary to move into past existence or past experiences in order to attempt to unravel the threads that have gone into the current belief system (as it projects into your pattern at this point in time), for you carry within you in this now, in this reality, within your own form, every experience. You need to go no further than this in order to reach a more objective state of beingness.*

All the patterns of our lives, both good and bad, were initially begun and empowered in our past lives. The negative patterns could have been hatched in traumatic events, abusive families, lives of hardship, or any number of causes. That first negative experience then creates a pattern made up of its thought forms, habits, and emotional blueprints. As each successive life follows, the pattern is continued by the parents giving birth to their child (the same pattern). We may never know exactly what caused a particular pattern to begin in the first place, but we don't have to know. We can still neutralize the *originating cause* of the pattern so that we don't recreate it again.

Every time you react because of an already established pattern, there are *ripple effects*, or consequences, of that action, as there are for all actions. These ripple effects move outward, widening the effect of the original pattern and further complicating and convoluting our lives.

Using guilt, I will illustrate how causes and ripple effects are important concepts to understand and to work into the Key Exercise.

Perhaps you lived in a tribal community when some explorers from a distant land arrived in your area. As they traveled through this New World, they came into contact with many local tribes, including yours. Let's say there was an outbreak of measles in the explorer's camp. While the explorers barely noticed the illness, since it was common for them, the local natives were hit hard because the disease was too new for them to build up immunity to it. Soon the measles spread through your tribe and wiped out 90% of the indigenous population.

Let's say that a week earlier you, a menstruating woman, had secretly crossed the local river at night to gather herbs to cure your dying mother. Even though you knew there was a tribal taboo forbidding any menstruating woman to enter the river, the situation's urgency outweighed your natural caution. The taboo was based on a tribal belief that if a woman did this, great harm would come to the tribe. Therefore, when the measles broke out the following week, killing most of your people, you mistakenly thought you were the cause. No one blamed you because no one knew you had been in the river. However, you knew. And as a result, in that lifetime you believed, beyond a shadow of a doubt, that you were responsible for all the deaths from the measles.

This could have been the life where guilt was born. The cause in this case was the misunderstanding within your culture about the disease, even though there was no intent to harm you or anyone. This misunderstanding resulted in the *false belief* (which you still carry at the etheric level) that you were responsible for all the deaths. As one of the few who lived through the massive epidemic, you obsessed over it for all your remaining days. Now the altered reality of guilt follows you and grows from lifetime to lifetime.

Every time you act out of guilt, there are ripple effects or consequences of that action. For example, in this lifetime, you have a friend that you were going to take to a party. At the last moment, there was a problem with your car and you knew it would delay you. So your friend had to go with someone else, and on the way there, they were in an accident. Even though you didn't cause the accident, you felt guilty because your car chose that moment to have problems. (Remember you have the emotional blueprint of guilt that is triggered even when you are not responsible.) Out of guilt, you gave your friend money to help with her bills while she recovered. And that was the money you had saved for your next semester in college. The ripple effects here are serious. You have to take out a loan to continue school, your friend is now feeling obligated to you, and you now resent her for your action (giving her the money), even though you don't admit it to yourself. Not only is the friendship between the two of you full of misunderstandings and potential problems that could end in the two of you parting ways, but you also have a loan to repay. This is an example of the ripple effects of the guilt pattern.

But now, years later, you have *become conscious*. You decide you want to neutralize that pattern since you often find yourself acting or reacting out of guilt. You don't remember the life during which guilt was born or what the cause was, nor do you have a complete understanding of what the many ripple effects could be. It doesn't matter. All you need to do when you call in guilt or any pattern is to neutralize *the causes and the ripple effects* of that pattern.

Chapter Nine: Getting Started

Higher Selves Quote

It is simplistic. Yet in this reality, it is often difficult to grasp—until you have worked with, become accustomed to, and practiced the exercise and the techniques—that you can change what you want to change and what you want to alter. You can do it. You're in a Free Will Kingdom.

****

Each soul is a snowflake. Each soul is responsible for its own totality. You are responsible for your wealth. No one else is responsible. You are responsible for your gifts and talents. No one else is responsible. You are responsible for your own destiny. No one else is responsible. You have chosen. And now it is time to begin to materialize outward, into your physical reality, the highest most positive frequency.

You begin by taking stock of the areas that you want to change. Look at your outer reality. What is it in your life you are not happy with? There are endless possibilities, and no two people will have the exact same issues or patterns. Right now just pick the one or two areas with which you are most unhappy and start there. Are you struggling financially? Feeling miserable with your job? Worrying about your weight? Are your relationships going poorly? Are you always in chaos? Are you chronically worried about what other people think of you? Are you afraid to meet new challenges? Are you overlooked/abandoned/judged by others more often than not?

I suggest you write your issues down. Keep this list handy, as you will be surprised by how long it may get over time. In addition, after you have worked on the first ones on the list, you will find you want to go back and work on them again. There are many layers to the deeper patterns, which will require more than one neutralization. The goal is to peel off these layers (by neutralizing them) in order to get all the way to the core of a pattern and to finally neutralize that. Even though consciously we want a pattern to change tomorrow at the unconscious level, the soul tends to hold on to it because it is familiar and part of its self-identity. Even a very negative pattern can feel comfortable if it has been around a long, long time. The pattern would be one that the soul is familiar with and, for which, has developed coping mechanisms. There can be great security in a known entity. Facing the unknown, however, not knowing what it will be like if that pattern dissolves, can be a scary place. So don't be concerned if you have to rework the same pattern several times. It is a normal part of the process. And you can work on fear of the unknown while you're at it!

As it clears out our etheric bodies of negative build-up, the soul/mind detox is a goal completely worthy of its effort. Every step helps, and more steps help even more. This is not about a finish-line mentality, where we think there will be no reward until we have gotten all the way to the end. Instead, this is a process that brings rewards at every stage. You will see new connections, new sides of issues, and new options that will open up as the energy streams/patterns move in new directions. Your emotional upheavals will begin to diminish, which is one of the most gratifying results. Overall, the life pattern will begin to shift. There will be small changes that initially may go unnoticed, but then you'll see them add up, becoming a new path that gains strength and momentum with more detox.

Please understand that the weaving process within the Creative Body is complex, involving dozens if not hundreds of thought forms, emotional blueprints and habit imprints, and is always in process. So, at first, you are building new weaves over old ones, resulting in shifts as you move forward. There is seldom an overnight, 180-degree change, even though the possibility of that is always there.

Let me give you an example. A friend of mine had a particularly problematic mother. Her mother was very controlling and could not see my friend (even into adulthood) as anything but a child she had to manage. Once my friend learned this Higher Self information, she began looking at her patterns. She saw that she pulled others into her life, including co-workers, friends, associates, and loved ones who often treated her in the same way as her mother. She would say to me, "I keep manifesting this pattern where people treat me like a child that has to be managed."

Once she began neutralizing the pattern and its related thought forms and habits, the energy began to shift. Not only did these mother mirrors come up less and less for her, but each time one did, she would work on neutralizing the pattern, getting to deeper and deeper levels. She also began to see other related patterns and worked on those too. She found that her reactions to the mother mirrors dramatically shifted.

She stopped being angry and frustrated with these people and blaming them for the way they treated her, and instead realized it didn't matter who they were. She had come to understand clearly that her energy identities magnetically attracted them into her life. So her anger dissipated, and on the odd occasion she came in contact with someone who in some small way was reflective of that mother, she just appreciated that the pattern had been brought to her consciousness, indicating that there were deeper layers still present. So work on them she did.

Today she no longer sees this recurring pattern. Did it take a week for her to do this? A month? No, it took a few years. But she was going to be a few years older anyway, so now she is older *and* has neutralized at least one of her major negative patterns. In addition, she is now closer to her mother than she ever was before.

The next chapter explains the Key Exercise as if I were leading you, the reader, through it in person. I did it this way to give you reminders of the material we've already covered. This way, you have the fuller context and understanding. You can read through this exercise on your own to get a feel for it, and/or you can have someone read it to you slowly, pausing here and there to give you time to process and focus on what is being said and on what you sense and experience.

At the end of the chapter, after explaining each step in more detail, I also give you the simple version you can use on a regular basis. Please make a copy of this version to use whenever it is convenient and when the book isn't around. In time you will remember it and you won't need the cheat sheet. You can always add elements of the longer version whenever you wish. I do various versions of the exercise myself, depending on the amount of time I have or the situation I'm in. When I work in a group, for example, we almost always do an extended version (though what is said varies each time), whereas when I work alone, I change it up depending on the focus at that moment.

Using the pattern of financial lack, which many of us want to change, the exercise is as follows…

Chapter Ten: The Key Exercise

Higher Selves Quote

Each of you has the power, ability and knowledge to take full and complete control of your life, to neutralize what you desire to neutralize, and create what you desire to create. Those who believe that they cannot and those who feel powerless to control their lives are those who are only blinded temporarily by the mask of the 4th Dimensional physical reality. You are capable. You are able. And you are ready.

CONSCIOUS MEDITATION

THE AMALGAMATION

Close your eyes and concentrate on the spark of Light within you while remembering that this Light is symbolic of the Pure Soul Essence carried within each of us. This Pure Soul Essence Light is our direct connection to the Originating Source and to all life. In this state of quiet, focus on your Light and allow it to grow, encompass and permeate every part of your being, every molecule of the physical body and the totality of your etheric bodies. As you center within your Light, amalgamate with and become the Light. Please take a moment and perceive the Light at whatever level you perceive. You may see it, you may imagine it, you may feel it, or you may sense it. It makes no difference. It is there. For a moment, I want you to experience this energy.

The Pure Soul Essence, this Light that you are, carries the power of the miraculous, the power of all knowledge and wisdom from the Highest Level. You are the perfection and the reflection of all that Originating Source was, is and is becoming. The Pure Soul Essence has within it everything you need in this reality to live at the very highest level of all your potentials. It is the purest, most perfect part within each individual soul, and by connecting to this symbol of Light, you are connecting to the Totality of All That Exists.

While centered within your Pure Soul Essence, I ask that you project into the Originating Source of All That Is. Thinking it, imagining it or intending it does this. Say, "I project into the Originating Source of All That Is." Again, take a moment to feel this energy. Now, in this state of consciousness, I also ask that you be amalgamated with all of your Higher Selves. To do this, think, "I am amalgamated with the Totality of my Higher Selves." Now, remain conscious at all levels: that you are standing within the center of your own Pure Soul Essence, standing as one with the Originating Source, amalgamated with the Totality of your Higher Selves, and that you are in this 4th Dimensional reality.

THE NEUTRALIZATION

From this place of centeredness and wholeness, I ask that you focus on the pattern of financial lack in your life. You have thought forms, habit imprints, and emotional blueprints that carry this pattern. It has manifested in your outer reality. There are areas within your physical body that are also affected by it. I now ask that you call forth the pattern of financial lack, consciously bringing all the energy identities forward in front of your mind's eye. Call in the parents and the children of all of the thoughts, habits, and blueprints that have created this pattern. Ask for all the energy identities, both directly and indirectly related to financial lack. Also, call in the causes and the ripple effects of the pattern. Circle all of them in a ring of light that holds them there in front of you. Say, "I surround all the energy identities with light." You do not have to see them or even sense them. Just say the words. You are amalgamated, and you are directing the Higher Selves to help you do this work in your Highest Ideal. Using the Light of your Pure Soul Essence, please send it into the ring of light to neutralize simultaneously all that is held there. The Light neutralizes the thought forms, erases and cauterizes (burns away) the habit imprints, and neutralizes the emotional blueprints.

Now, please have your Light engulf and absorb all that you have neutralized. This guarantees that the neutral energy will benefit you. Simultaneously, also direct your Light in, through and around your physical body, asking that it move into any and all areas also affected by financial lack, bringing healing and perfection to any area in need of it. Feel the energy as it penetrates into all the molecules, organs, and systems of your physical being and bathes you with its perfection and balance.

THE EMPOWERMENT

I now ask that you call forth the thought form of financial abundance, imagine it to be in front of you, and enclose it in a circle of light. First amalgamate this energy identity with your Higher Selves so the thought form operates in your Highest Ideal at all times. Simply saying, "I amalgamate financial abundance with the Higher Selves" does this. Remember that even what we consider positive thought forms can combine in unexpected ways with negative ones to create a weave of an unwanted situation or condition. Now send the Light of your Pure Soul Essence into this thought form and visualize, imagine or sense financial abundance growing and expanding as big as you feel comfortable with—there is no limit set, no restrictions required. You have now changed the balance between financial lack and financial abundance.

End of Meditation

A Step-by-Step Explanation of the Exercise

In order to clarify the exercise, I have broken it down into eight steps. Keep in mind that any pattern/s can be used with this exercise even though I used financial lack/abundance in my example.

One: I am one with my Pure Soul Essence Light, and I ask that it fully encompass the totality of my physical body and my etheric bodies.

Here you focus on the Pure Soul Essence, that spark of Light from the Originating Source, as it fills every nook and cranny in the physical and etheric bodies, bringing to them its perfection, balance and harmony. If you have trouble connecting to the symbol of the spark of Light, you can try seeing yourself within the diamond-shaped symbol described earlier in Chapter Two. Both work. You can contact this point of power any time you desire simply by focusing your attention on either one of these symbols or just by saying the words, "I am one with my Pure Soul Essence."

Two: I become one with the Originating Source of All There Is.

The Source of All Life is a creator without gender that is in a state of creating all the time. Its energy—the Creative Life Force—processes through each individual vehicle of expression (each soul). Because every soul is connected to the Originating Source at all times by its Pure Soul Essence, we have access to the Totality of all the Divine Energy, Wisdom and Knowledge. By amalgamating with the Originating Source, we are consciously tapping into that unimaginably expansive power.

Three: I am amalgamated with the Totality of my Higher Selves

Not only do the Higher Selves add an important level of protection, but also since we are in the Free Will Kingdom, we have to ask them to be part of the process in order to receive their help. Their energy can be intense, and your mind may stray as you do the work. That happens less and less as you get used to it. When you find your thoughts wandering, just pull your focus back in and continue. You can also work directly on thought forms related to difficulty focusing, which helps in many other areas of life as well.

When you amalgamate with the Pure Soul Essence, the Originating Source and/or the Higher Selves, do you have any sensations? Can you feel the energy or sense it in any way? If not, you can ask the Higher Selves to intensify the Amalgamation. Keep in mind that what you are doing is happening whether or not you sense or see anything. Some people will get a sense of these energies immediately and others will not. Either way, you are equally effective at doing the work. You may find yourself questioning the process, and that is normal. If doubt takes over, you can take a deep breath, amalgamate, and start again. (You can also neutralize self-doubt as well!) It can be frustrating if you are someone who sees, hears or senses nothing. I was like that for a very long time. I encourage you to take a leap of faith and give the process a chance, since you will find change happens anyway. In time, whether sooner or later, you will experience the powerful energy.

Four: I call forth the pattern of _______________ (any one you wish to work on)—the 'parents' and 'children' the causes and effects, the indirect and direct thought forms, habit imprints, and emotional blueprints, and encircle them in a ring of light.

This step is straightforward. You are asking that all the imprints, blueprints, and thought forms related to an issue or pattern come forward. Surrounding them in a circle of light holds them in one group and facilitates the neutralizing process. Therefore, when you send your Light in, as is done in the next step, it is addressing exactly what you want to work on. By focusing on a certain pattern, you are infusing your work with the conscious energy of intent. You can also call in broad categories of patterns rather than specific ones. For example, you can work on all fears (rather than just the fear of snakes, for example), doubts, stress factors, control issues—whatever is bothering you most in that moment.

FIVE: I direct the Light of my Pure Soul Essence to neutralize the pattern of _________________ in my physical body and all the etheric bodies simultaneously.

Once you have called out the pattern you want to neutralize, you then ask that your Light neutralize all of the thought forms, habits and emotional blueprints in the etheric bodies and to heal all effects of that pattern in the physical body. Again, you do this by thinking it, seeing it or feeling it, whatever method works best for you. The thought forms will be neutralized; the habit imprints cauterized and the emotional blueprint's Velcro will be inactivated. And if there is related physical issues that need healing, those will be addressed as well.

Let me give you an example of how a friend of mine does his neutralizing. John has a great imagination, and he has inspired me as well. After he amalgamates, he asks that the Habit, Thought Form, and Emotional Response Bodies join together to become a conglomerate body. He then calls forth the thought forms, habit imprints and emotional blueprints for one pattern at a time or for multiple patterns, seeing/imagining them (with his eyes closed) in front of him. When there are a slew of them, he shoots out his Pure Soul Essence Light, pulsating like a supernova. After he zaps the first wave, he regroups for a few seconds, calls for more, and then shoots out the Light again. His Light neutralizes the thought forms, cauterizes the habit imprints and dissolves the emotional blueprints simultaneously. It then absorbs all the neutralized energy. The Light never gets used up, but at some point he feels it is enough and stops.

Does he follow the steps I've outlined exactly? No. And that is all right. If you are amalgamated you are working out of the Divine Will pattern that will only work in your Highest Ideal. John made changes to the work after he had done it for a while in the way I have instructed here. In time, he was comfortable enough to find his own way and did so. I encourage you to work with the exercise as I have explained here a few times first before making any changes, however, when amalgamated you can make changes that work for you. You can use John's method or find your own unique method. You can imagine it happening, think it happening, or feel it happening. As long as you are amalgamated, you will be protected.

Six: I ask that my Light engulf and absorb the neutralized energy.

This step is to absorb the neutralized energy into your Light. When neutralized, the energy has been rendered harmless. And at that point it is available for use. We therefore absorb it to empower our Light.

Seven: I call forth the (positive) thought form of ____________ (the opposite of what you neutralized) and I amalgamate it with my Higher Selves.

When amalgamating the positive thought form with the Higher Selves, you guarantee that a positive thought form will be working in your highest ideal. Everything that is manifested, even the negative patterns, has positive thought forms that are part of the weave that creates your outer reality. I remind you of the example of Josh and his job-loss pattern and his underlying belief that he was a better father than a provider. This belief could have easily been part of a weave that may have caused him to lose his job. So amalgamating every positive thought form that we create or empower with the Higher Selves is imperative. Due to the great complexity of our creations, let's have the Higher Selves ensure that the positive thought forms we are empowering will only be used to create and manufacture our lives in our Highest Ideal.

Sometimes it may be difficult to know exactly what the opposite is for a negative pattern. You do not have to be able to name it. As I will explain in the next chapter, you can use the prefix 'un' to signify the opposite of the negative thought form you've neutralized (sorrow, un-sorrow)

Eight: I send my Light into my Thought Form Body to empower the thought form of _________________.

At this point, we send in the Light to grow the positive thought form to be as large as you want/need/can imagine. The more powerful it is, the faster the magnetic energy will bring the actual manifestation into our outer reality. When I do the empowering, I imagine my positive thought forms as becoming so huge that I can no longer see their edges. They grow way beyond my field of vision. There are no limits.

Multiple Patterns

You can also neutralize multiple patterns at the same time. I often go in and call forth five to ten patterns at once because they may be related to a larger pattern. For example, when I worked on a shoulder problem related to repetitive motion on the computer, I came at it from many different directions. I began by working on neutralizing the injury of the shoulder, and then called in all etheric patterns that might be affecting it. In this case, I called in aging patterns (including bone loss) and burden patterns—either being a burden or carrying a burden—as it seemed possible that they could be related. This then took me to neutralizing disability patterns, avoidance patterns (could there be a reason why I am inviting the shoulder problem, that it keeps me from doing something I am unconsciously afraid of?) and/or issues of flexibility and/or restriction.

In short, once you get going on something, please feel free to expand the exercise to wherever it takes you. You don't have to know if you have any of the issues that come up for you, but if they pop into your mind, the chances are that they are there somewhere. They could be relatively minor or seemingly non-existent in this life, but since there is no telling what has happened to us before, it is always worth calling out and neutralizing whatever comes to mind, using your own intuition.

Duration and Frequency

How long does the exercise take and how often should you do it? To start, you may find yourself taking 20 to 30 minutes to get through the exercise once in order to focus and experience it all. After a few sessions, however, you'll find you can easily cut the time in half. The Amalgamation will flow quickly, and then you can move through the neutralizations and empowerments. This doesn't mean that you can't take longer, especially when you want to work on many patterns at once. You just stay in the process and call out whatever you wish. You can also do the exercise in short bursts, while grabbing a few minutes in the shower, washing dishes, while muting the TV ads, and/or while you are on that boring treadmill. This way, you are multitasking by doing two positive things for yourself at once! It is important, though, to focus on what you are doing. If after a while you're doing it like you are on automatic pilot, reciting words, it becomes less and less effective. It is important to focus your thoughts and to be consciousness while you work.

I recommend again that you copy the exercise and put it up in several key places in your apartment/home/office, such as the bedroom, bathroom, den, garage, or your wallet. Then it's handy to use when you find yourself with a little time. Before long, you will remember the words and will not need the reminder.

The Higher Selves recommend doing the exercise every day. Even the most dedicated of you will find that you will do it in fits and starts. Please do not feel that you are a failure in some way if you are inconsistent. This is the norm, and Rome wasn't built in a day. Of course, the more you do it the more you will progress. When you are in crisis, you may find you are doing it several times a day, and when things are going smoothly, you might forget to do it more than once a week. Everyone will develop a pattern that works for him/her.

Action Is Required

You need to continue to take action in your life. This is not about doing the key exercise and then sitting on the couch, waiting for news that you're the lucky winner of a car/money/job/any pie-in-the-sky windfall. Long ago, in a reading, the Higher Selves told someone in Joan's group that he would become a famous actor. When nothing happened after six months, he went back to Joan to find out why. "Are you taking acting classes?" she asked. "No," he said. "Are you going out on auditions?" "No." "What are you doing then?" And he said, "Sitting by the phone, waiting for the call that offers me the part that will make me famous." Today, he laughs at himself and understands that he must be the creator of his own opportunities. Joan had been reading the probabilities in his Creative Body. By not taking action, he changed the probabilities and did not manifest that reality. Therefore, please continue to make the effort to help yourself. By doing so, along with the additional soul/mind detox work presented in *CHOICES*, it will enable you to be successful.

Results

So what exactly can you expect from doing this exercise? Working to neutralize your financial lack and empowering your financial abundance, for example, doesn't mean you will find a check in your mailbox the next day. Focused work with this may manifest a raise, a new job opportunity, a loan, cost-cutting discoveries, or maybe an opportunity to upgrade your skills, leading to higher pay on the job. Every person will manifest the shift in different ways. Be aware of what is happening or you might miss an open door. It is also possible that an answer or solution will present itself, but if it comes from a direction that is unexpected, you might not even see it immediately. You also might not realize that an opportunity, though not the immediate answer or solution is actually the first step. Just to be safe, you can also work on removing any blinders you may have on, so that awareness will come in along with the shift. As you continue the work, the shift will gain momentum, moving you to material balance.

Another powerful result of the exercise is that you will find yourself feeling better inside. There will be less emotional upheaval and more hope for a solution. You might even find that your perspective on your financial lack shifts. You may begin to see that even though you have some financial lack, you are more receptive to appreciating the richness you have in other areas. Self-confidence may also be a result (either subtly or significantly) and/or over time your demeanor may change, eliciting positive responses that are new to you. It is a process and an effective one that manifests itself differently for each individual. It is best not to lock into one result because that one result may not manifest exactly as you expect. This could lead to feelings of failure when, in fact, you are on your way to success, even if the path doesn't take the route you had planned. If possible, stand in the center of expectation, and allow the results to take you where they may, while knowing that these results are going to be in your Highest Ideal.

Doing the Exercise on your Own

Here is the exercise laid out again. Now that you've read through the process I gave you at the beginning of the chapter and the descriptions of each step, I ask that you choose another pattern you want to work on most and try it yourself using the words below. You can do it.

THE KEY EXERCISE

THE AMALGAMATION

I am one with my Pure Soul Essence Light, and I ask that it fully encompass the totality of my physical body and my etheric bodies.

I become one with the Originating Source of All There Is.

I am amalgamated with the Totality of my Higher Selves.

THE NEUTRALIZATION

I call forth the pattern of ______________—the parents and children, the causes and effects, the indirect and direct thought forms, habit imprints and emotional blueprints—and encircle them in a ring of light.

I direct the Light of my Pure Soul Essence to neutralize ________________ in my physical body and all the etheric bodies simultaneously.

I ask that my Light engulf and absorb the neutralized energy.

THE EMPOWERMENT

I call forth the (positive) thought form of ____________ (the opposite of what you neutralized) and I amalgamate it with my Higher Selves.

I send my Light into my Thought Form Body to empower the thought form of __________________.

End of exercise.

Repeat the Exercise of the Neutralization and Empowerment

Now that you've tried the exercise once on your own, try it again using yet another pattern. For example, one many of us have in common is illness. Whether it is illness, weight problems, guilt or bad luck, try a few in a row to get the hang of it. Remember that it is not about using the exact words. You may not remember them perfectly and you may add something of your own, using a symbol that works for you. That is perfectly fine *as long as you are amalgamated and working in the Divine Will frequency* of your Pure Soul Essence.

As you read through more of the chapters, you'll be learning more exercises. You can practice one chapter at a time or several chapters at once. Feel free to move at your own speed.

Chapter Eleven: Experiencing Your Etheric Bodies

Higher Selves Quote

The bottom line is each of us is only a host for these altered realities that live in our Thought Form Bodies…they are the boss and we are the host.

When we learned the neutralizing technique from the Higher Selves in the original Wednesday group, they first taught us to go into each etheric body one by one to do the work. This had the benefit of giving us the experience with each body, to sense the energies present, and to help us understand how the process works. However, in time, they had us see the envelopes (fields) of energy as a conglomerate body, one that we could address all at once. And that's the way we've done it since and the way I explained it to you in the previous chapter. It is still important that you understand how the Light of your Pure Soul Essence actually does the neutralizations. It is also an interesting opportunity to experience each Body. Therefore, in this chapter I am inviting you on a journey into the etheric space around you, to see what you see, and to help you better understand the parts of ourselves that create our lives.

The Thought Form Body

Close your eyes and, as with all exercises, first do the Amalgamation. Then starting with the Thought Form Body, I ask that you imagine yourself there by simply stating, "I project into my Thought Form Body (or Habit Body or Emotional Body)." (This is the same as picturing you on the beach in Hawaii or visualizing you going through a routine on a balance beam.) With that thought, you will consciously project inside of your Thought Form Body.

You may experience it as a large space with many thought forms floating/looming/crowding around you. Or you may see/sense nothing. That is okay. If you don't experience anything, I recommend that after working with the Key Exercise for a month or three, you try again. You may be surprised by how much your perceptions have opened up. Keep in mind at all times that these energy identities are both soulless and mindless and cannot hurt you. It is possible (though unlikely) that at times they may feel frightening or overwhelming. What turns up in your own unconscious may surprise you. If something unsettling appears, simply imagine it smaller in size or direct it to turn around so you see it from the back instead—anything that makes you feel more comfortable. Also, encasing it in Light will contain it and will take away the menacing factor.

Using the thought form of poor body image as the example in this chapter, call this thought form forward. It will present itself as an actual dark shape, the form of which is completely determined by each individual. It could be human in shape—male, female or androgynous—with a miserable demeanor, showing its body looking the way you negatively think about yourself: overweight/ underweight, hips too big/small, legs to short/long, and so on. It could also look like a dark amorphous blob, or anything else. There is no exact description I can give you since each person has his/her own unique thought patterns, which are reflected in the appearance of each thought form.

In addition, you can converse with a thought form to find out more about it—when it began, where it lives, the conditions it lives in, etc. Remember that thought forms create their own *altered realities.* Therefore, you may see the environment in which it lives, such as a dark cave, an overcrowded space or some type of room. If you are someone who can hear or sense this altered reality, you will be amazed at what you can discover about your past—this lifetime and others. I only know a few people who can actually get much more than a sense of these energy identities, but just knowing you can ask questions may lead any one of you to explore an area you might not have thought of before. And who knows, you may find you have a talent for this.

Neutralizing a Thought Form

The following is what happens in the Thought Form Body during the neutralization process of energy identities. Each and every thought form carries its symbolic opposite—an imaginary but very real outline equal in size and shape to the thought form, but an outline that is completely empty. For all negative thought forms (for clarity's sake) using the term 'un' before the negative term will denote this opposite. For example, hate's opposite, instead of being love, is un-hate. So the poor body image's opposite will be the un-poor body image. I do this for two reasons: First, it can be difficult to name the opposite energy for some thought forms, so this keeps it simple. Second, it's important to clarify that when we're neutralizing hate, for example, it doesn't mean that we are losing our love thought form in the process. The neutralization of any negative thought form brings a state of balance, resulting in its neutrality to that thought form. It does not, however, take away the positive thought forms to do so. So when we neutralize hate, love is still in existence in the Thought Form Body. Of course, if you can name the opposite of a thought form, you may certainly use it instead of 'un'.

When we direct the Pure Soul Essence Light to neutralize the thought form of poor body image, it fills that empty outline with the lighted opposite energy (un-poor body image), becoming a mirror image equal in size and shape to the negative dark thought form. Your Light then merges the two equal parts (black and white merge to become the neutral gray) and thus the poor body image thought form is neutralized. The Light then goes on to absorb this gray energy, adding that energy to itself—your Pure Soul Essence.

While you are projected into the Thought Form Body, I suggest you take time to actually neutralize and absorb your poor body image thought form (the parents and children, the causes and effects, and the direct and indirect) and see/sense what happens. While fully amalgamated with your Higher Selves, call on your Pure Soul Essence Light to process the neutralization of your poor body image. See the thought form and the opposite outline. Using the Light, fill that outline until the un-poor body image matches the poor body image. Now consciously see the two opposites merge to become one. You have neutralized this negative thought form.

While you are there, if you think of any specific negative judgments you know you have in the poor body image area, please call those in as well, such as "I hate my hair/figure/looks" or "I'm not as strong/well-built/put together as I want to be." We find endless ways to attack and judge our physical bodies. All these judgments hold us prisoner as they add power to the fuel that attracts unwelcome situations and conditions. While they are there, they magnetically pull in situations and conditions that will continue to fuel those beliefs.

The Habit Body

Now project into the Habit Body by simply thinking, "I project into my Habit Body." You can do this by projecting from the Thought Form Body directly into the Habit Body. This body is often experienced as a large expanse with ruts or grooves marring the landscape. If you don't see this, it doesn't mean you're doing it wrong. Not sensing anything at all, or sensing something completely different, only reflects how unique you are, carrying your own viewpoints and symbols. Now call forth the imprints for poor body image. You may have intense ingrained ruts, or you may have a small field of grooves. Again, each individual determines the depth and size of the habit imprint of poor body image. While everyone in some way has this thought form and habit imprint, the intensity of it varies widely.

To neutralize these (or any) imprints, we always use the Pure Soul Essence Light. You can think of the Light as cauterizing the wrinkled landscape, burning away the deep wrinkles, as would a laser on aging skin. The image of water washing over lumps in the sand, smoothing them out as it returns to sea, is also effective. I personally see it almost like an eraser on a blackboard erasing chalk lines. There is no right way, only the way in which you feel comfortable. Since the habit imprints and the thought forms work together, it is essential to work on both for every pattern. Don't forget that now that you have called forth the habit imprints, you need to cauterize them. Please take this time to send in your Light to neutralize the poor body image imprints.

The Emotional Body

Projecting into the Emotional Body is an interesting and sometimes weird experience. Yet, you do so in exactly the same way as the other Bodies, saying, "I project into my Emotional

Body." When I project in, I often see the blueprints as huge heavy mounds or blobs of yuck—for lack of a better word. And when I work on my blueprints, sometimes I see great movement, and other times it's as if they are so hardened I can barely get them to loosen up. I encourage you, though, not to give up. These difficult ones may seem hard-wired, but they do eventually unravel and become neutralized. One technique is to intensify the Light (just by asking) and send it in symbolically as dynamite or a laser beam. There is nothing in there that you are unable to neutralize, even if it takes time.

To neutralize the blueprints associated with poor body image, we send our Pure Soul Essence Light in to dissolve the glue that holds our negative responses to the event triggering negative judgments. Maybe you are trying on clothes that don't seem to fit, and you think, "If only I had a smaller waist or a bigger bust, they might actually look okay." Then the emotional responses kick in, perhaps bringing up feelings of disgust (why can't I be more disciplined about a diet?) or anger (how can I be expected to look good when my life is so hard, and I never have time to work on myself?) or despair (will I ever be able to enjoy shopping when just looking at myself in the mirror is so awful?). There may also be responses that are not so obvious. Of course you could request that specific blueprints be neutralized if you know right away that frustration or guilt or anything else comes up every time the poor body image pattern is in play. So, also ask that every emotional blueprint to be neutralized, known or unknown, which may be part of it.

Now that you have the idea, I suggest that you take this moment to close your eyes, re-amalgamate if you need to, project into your Emotional Body, and see what it's like. Please focus on neutralizing those poor body image blueprints that have haunted you (and most everyone else) for long enough.

Once again, it is important to remember that we are not neutralizing the emotions themselves but rather the attachments holding the emotional responses, the Velcro/glue that has created the blueprints.

From time to time, as you neutralize your emotional response patterns, either by working on them in the conglomerate or by doing it directly from within the Emotional Body, you may experience the actual emotion of the pattern. If you do, just continue to send in the Light and allow the emotional response to process through you and outward. See it as dark smoke going out of the top of your head and turning white as it hits the air. This is the best way to process any emotional reaction, and it goes a long way in preventing us from overreactions, mood swings and high-drama moments. Of course, what's most important is that we'll just plain feel better!

Thought Form Body Revisited

Before you finish, I suggest that you once again project into your Thought Form Body in order to empower the positive body image thought form. Once there, call forth this energy identity and again pay attention to what you may see or experience. You may find that this thought form is large, small or virtually nonexistent. Personally, I found that many of my positive thought forms were incredibly small when compared to my huge, off the charts negative ones. At first it was disheartening, but when I saw how quickly the Light empowered them, I was not at all worried about it. Of course, be sure to be in the amalgamated state as you go through this process. Ask that your Higher Selves be amalgamated with the positive body image thought form in order to keep it working in your Highest Ideal. Then send the Pure Soul Essence Light into the thought form. Watch or imagine the thought form grow until it is as huge as you want it to be. This may give you a sense of accomplishment and hope.

The Physical Body

Finally, I suggest you concentrate on sending your Light into, throughout and around your physical body. You can direct it to the area/s that you are least happy with, asking what needs neutralizing be neutralized and what needs healing be healed. The Pure Soul Essence carries balance and perfection, which can be brought to those areas and to the whole body in your Highest Ideal. You won't wake up 20 pounds lighter the next day, but with regular use of the energy in the body, as well as taking the actions required, you will see changes, the first of which will be a greater acceptance of your outward physical expression.

Last Note

There is no problem if you choose to do the Key Exercise in each Body separately instead of using the simultaneous process. However, be sure to address the pattern/issue/belief in each of your etheric bodies instead of doing it piecemeal, e.g., one day you do the thought form and a week later you do the blueprint. These three bodies reinforce and recreate each other on a moment-to-moment basis, so it is important that you neutralize the patterns in all of them in one sitting, or you will find yourself repeating work more often than necessary.

Chapter Twelve: Working With Your Creative Body

Higher Selves Quote

The Creative Body contains records of the totality of all that you are, were and can be. It also contains records of the totality of all your experiences, past and present, in all forms and all dimensions and on all planets. It can, therefore, be utilized as a planning room. It can also be used as a symbol to link individuals to the resources of their totality. Past experiences can be viewed. Talents can be identified, and positive solutions can be created and applied to current difficult situations. The Creative Body can be scanned, and through the scanning process, an area of discord can be picked up that has not yet manifested in the outer reality. This condition can then be healed in the etheric, preventing it from ever manifesting.

Understanding and using the Creative Body to consciously create what you want for your outer reality is a powerful tool. You learned in Chapter Six that this Body is where your life is manufactured through the weaving process of the Creative Life Force energy. It is the place, therefore, that houses all potential creations (manifestations) we are building before they become strong enough to manifest. Even though it may seem like science fiction, wouldn't it be incredible to be able to project into the Creative Body, find the creations that we don't want, and then stop the creation from manifesting in our lives? And equally, wouldn't it be thrilling to find good things that are in process and somehow be able to either speed up their manifestation or add to their richness? Of course, as an idea, it would be fantastic. Is it doable? Yes. The Higher Selves have clearly explained exactly how you can decide your own future.

Scanning the Creative Body

To begin, I would like you to think of a question you have about something in your life for which you don't have an answer. It can be something about your work (will my project/presentation be successful/well received?), something about a relationship (how will the conflict/disagreement I am having with my spouse end up?), about your destiny (what path am I on and how is it going?) or about your finances (will I ever make enough money so that I can buy that car I always wanted/go on that trip/go back to school/retire?). Any question works, and you are your own best guide on this.

When you are ready to give this a try, sit quietly and close your eyes. (In time you may be able to do some of this work without closing your eyes, but it helps one to focus.) As with every exercise, please amalgamate with your Pure Soul Essence, the Originating Source, and with your Higher Selves. This will not only afford you protection, ensuring that you won't do any harm, but you may also get information from the Higher Selves while you're in the Creative Body that can help you understand what you're seeing. You may ask about any energy weave that is about to play itself out. The Pure Soul Essence Light will also be utilized to make the changes you want.

To start – project yourself into the envelope of energy (the energy field) of the Creative Body in the same manner that you did with your other etheric bodies. Say, "I project into my Creative Body." Take some time to experience this energy field and to become comfortable with it. This Body contains the potential creations that are initialized at the thought form level and reinforced at the habit and emotional levels. You may pick up several patterns of potential creations, but for the time being, please try not to be sidetracked since you have a specific search to do. You are going to look for the answer to your question. Move through your Creative Body and be open, without judgment, about what you are or are not receiving. Search for that part within your Creative Body that holds the potential outward manifestation related to your question.

Many of you will be entirely convinced that you will never be able to read your Creative Body, least of all this first time. I assure you that this is not true. Some will do this very well, and others will have a harder time. And if you can't do it, don't judge yourself as a failure, screw-up, or less of a person compared to the person who can. Perceiving at these etheric levels can take time to develop. Like any other muscle, it needs to be used. Some people have already developed the talent either in this life, past lives or both. They will move into this type of perception more easily than those who have developed other gifts and talents. Yet just because you haven't done this before, it doesn't mean you can't develop the ability now. As one who didn't have this ability at first, I found it difficult to tap into those elusive energy fields. Yet, I can assure you that it will happen for all who practice. It helps to neutralize the patterns of self-doubt and/or fear and/or any number of reasons/beliefs that are standing in your way. For now, stand between belief and disbelief, put any distractions aside, and continue looking for your answer.

When you find the energy weave that is being manufactured, the potential weave that answers your question, see what it looks like. If you can't see it, you may get a sense of it. Do the best you can. Once you've connected with it, you have a decision to make. Are you satisfied with this potential creation?

Is this what you want the end result to be? Decide yes or no. Yes, I do want it. Or no, I do not.

Making the Change

Keeping in mind that the Thought Form Body, Habit Body, and Emotional Body are actually housed within the Creative Body, you can now use your Pure Soul Essence Light to make the changes you want. If you are unhappy with the potential creation, you can neutralize the thought forms, habits and blueprints that are fueling that negative weave. Remember that multiple thought forms could be part of the creation. Call for all of them simultaneously, whether known or unknown. In other words, you may not know exactly what energy identities are empowering it. This makes no difference since your Higher Selves will make sure the correct ones are present. Place a ring of energy around them so they are the focal point. Then send in your Light to neutralize and absorb those energy identities. If, on the other hand, you are happy with the developing creation, then you can proceed as above, but instead, send in your Light to empower the thought forms responsible. Do remember (as always) to amalgamate those thought forms with the Higher Selves.

I would like to admit that at first I did not utilize this tool as much as I could have. In the beginning, when the information was brought it, I worked a lot with the exercise but was disappointed I could not see any of my potential creations. My ability to see and sense was unavailable to me at the time. After a while, I gave up. And for many, many years I never tried it again. However, I knew the information was vital and important to share. My thinking was that, even if only a small percentage of readers had the ability to utilize this tool, I needed to offer it. Therefore, because I didn't want to write about something with which I had no first-hand experience, I decided to try again. And what a difference two decades made!

This time, I projected into the Creative Body and immediately saw and sensed a lot going on. I figured out that while I hadn't worked with this particular exercise, I had worked hard at developing my psychic powers and my ability to pull in the Higher Self information. As a result, this exercise is now doable for me. And I wish I hadn't waited so long to try it again! That's why I'm encouraging each reader to go back periodically to try this, or anything else, since you will find that you can become more and more perceptive about this etheric energy.

My Experience with the Creative Body

In order for you to have at least some reference point, I would like to share the start of my recent experience. The first time I tried it, I didn't ask a question, since I didn't think I'd see the answer. So I projected into the Creative Body and there, right in front of me, was a '*me*' in a female energy form, a potential creation in the making. This 'me' was hanging, as if suspended in the air, with Light and colors swirling around.

Every second or two, some ball of energy would come out of various directions and shoot across the expanse, looking as if it was being sucked into the creation by some giant vacuum. And each ball became part of this 'me,' adding to the pure energy swirling around it. It was amazing. I felt the intensity of the creation and could see all the energy that was going into it. And I had no idea what the creation was! I tried to get the information, but all I knew was that it was positive. I then called in all the thought forms, habits, and blueprints that were a part of it, amalgamated all of them with the Higher Selves, and sent my Light in to add more energy. And that seemed enough for my first try.

When I went in the next time, I immediately saw the 'me' from the previous attempt, and it had grown immensely. It was huge as a result of the energy I had used to empower all the positive thought forms, etc. That felt great, even though I didn't know exactly what it was yet. I decided to look around to see what else I could find, and so my field of vision shifted. Right beside the female 'me' was a male energy form in the same exact size as the female. Again, I didn't know what it meant. But I also knew it was positive.

There was a balance between the two forms that felt exactly right. Both were growing and gaining strength, and the sense I had was that the simultaneous creation was truly in my Highest Ideal. I wasn't sure if it meant I was bringing balance to the male and female within my beingness, or whether it meant I was going to manifest an equal partner in a love relationship or a work situation, but it was okay that I didn't know. What I did know was that is was a good thing.

Shortly thereafter, I went in again in an attempt to learn more, and there was this dark, murky kind of energy that had no specific characteristics. It felt as if it wasn't fully formed yet, and it didn't feel good at all. I immediately called in the thought forms, habits, and blueprints that were part of its creation, and I began to neutralize them. As I sent in the Light, this potentially negative creation began to get smaller and smaller, and then it just disappeared. I was amazed. I asked the Higher Selves what it was, and they explained that in this case, it was unnecessary for me to know. That to know might only result in worry or concern, which might cause its rebirth. So I let that one go like a hot potato.

Now I go in on a more regular basis, and even though I'm still learning, I am progressing a little at a time. It can be extremely helpful even if you only partially understand what you're getting. I encourage you to work with this planning room. By sitting down and literally reading your own Creative Body, you can become your own best psychic, and, more than that, you can take control over what you manifest.

Part 3

RESOLVING CHALLENGES ALONG THE WAY

Chapter Thirteen: Emotionalizing

Higher Selves Quote

When we learn to become conscious of any emotion that we are emotionalizing (which means that we must reach a point of acting on the emotion rather than reacting to the emotion) we will then be able to more easily reach that state of centering. At this point the emotion can be whatever it is, but it won't affect us in the pure expression of who we really are.

What exactly is *emotionalizing*? It's when we are caught up in an emotional upheaval, feeling rage, despair, fear or even the excitement of love. It's not when you are calmly sitting on the other side of the emotion rationally looking at it or discussing it with someone.

Although we emotionalize both positive and negative emotions, this chapter will focus on the negative examples, since these are the ones that are the most debilitating. There are positive emotions that don't serve us well either (such as the high or excitement felt when gambling, which can lead to an overindulgence), so what is explained here is equally valid for some positive emotions.

Understanding and processing emotions properly is challenging. The time when we need to be most aware and mindful of an activated emotion is most likely when we're already caught up in the whirlwind of pain, sorrow, anger or hurt. Emotions can be so powerful that we lose ourselves to them. Is this a good thing? No. Is there a way to deal with them? Yes. Let's find out how.

What Happens When We Emotionalize

Your co-worker has just taken full credit for the solution you came up with for your company's sales slump. You just found out your spouse is cheating on you. Your best chance at getting the money you were desperate for is subverted by an arrogant loan officer. And so on. In each case, a whirlwind of emotional anger, frustration, hurt, fear or confusion hits you like a ton of bricks. It can pick you up like a tornado and hold you in its grip as it spins out of control.

Keeping your mind on anything else is almost impossible since the emotional responses dominate your focus. Your mind loses its ability to think rationally or calmly—even when you think you have more clarity than ever. In fact, finding answers and solutions is most often difficult just when it's often most important. Also, you might behave in a way that you fully regret after the emotion has passed. Emotionalizing can also drain your energy and cause fatigue. It can unleash toxins within the physical body. The emotional state of an individual is the single most important factor in how one views his/her outer reality, as well as how well he/she handles it.

Emotional Targeting

When we are in the middle of a triggered emotional response, our first reaction is to cast blame on the person who was involved. Your teenager deliberately refused to do what he was told, resulting in serious consequences—and this makes you angry. Your boss heavily criticized your efforts on a project, humiliating you in front of your coworkers. Your friend told you that your advice/insight/so-called help was no longer welcome and walked away from the friendship, making you feel worthless. In each case, you target (focus) your emotional responses fully on the individual who caused your misery. And you feel completely justified to judge that person. Your teenager is too stubborn for his own good. Your boss is a jerk and wouldn't know a good thing if it hit him in the face. Your friend/ex-friend was more selfish than anything else, so who cares. You feel blameless, so your focus is on the other person, the target. This type of reaction is so much a part of the human condition that most people would look at it as completely normal. However, even if this is the type of response we often expect of others, or ourselves, it doesn't mean it's the best option. And I think you know why.

You will recall that we carry emotional blueprints from hundreds of thousands of lifetimes. (See Chapter Five.) So when someone gets us riled up emotionally, he/she is in fact only the trigger that releases our programmed emotional responses. Additionally, this event (and the person involved) could not have happened to us if we hadn't manufactured it first. Each of us is the creator of our own outer reality. So, to blame the other person, though it seems normal, is, in fact, erroneous. We all do so because we haven't understood the process. Now, we can see that we brought the incident into our lives. Blaming the other person will only continue to empower the energy identities that were part of the weave that manufactured the condition in the first place. Our emotional targeting generates powerful thought forms of judgment. The Habit imprints are deepened, and the emotional blueprints are reinforced. We are locking ourselves further into a cycle of repetition.

To further clarify, I need to point out that both individuals created the situation. The very person we're convinced is wrong and who we feel justified blaming also finds his/her action or reaction justifiable. So, the teenager felt that by ignoring his parents' request, he was letting them know he can make decisions on his own. The boss truly felt your work was so poor, that criticizing you in front of others was his way of making an impact on you. And the friend felt so patronized by you that, despite knowing you were only trying to be helpful, she felt her only choice was to walk away. Whether the justifications were right or wrong makes no difference and is irrelevant. Each person was playing a role in the problem, and both felt justified in blaming the other. Neither person is right or wrong. Both parties were led into this situation by their own unconscious weaves from lifetimes of thought forms and emotional blueprints, which were created by heavy layers of misunderstanding. And both sides will continue to create and recreate similar situations in their lives, unless they become conscious and address the emotionalizing properly.

Therefore, when we seek out a person or a situation as a target, and focus an emotion on that person/situation, we take what should have been a pure and simple emotional response (with a beginning, middle and end) and *cement* it in such a way that we carry it around for a long time. It will empower not only the chance of it happening again, but it will also increase the intensity of the response. These blueprints that we carry around comprise our emotional baggage. You may not realize it, but that response you just had to the driver who cut you off carries with it the fury and rage of *all* the injustices you've experienced up to that point.

Clearly, targeting an emotion by blaming someone else is not a good thing. Yet there will also be instances where you will be unable to determine what is causing an emotion. You wake up feeling irritable, or you can't seem to shake the feeling of doom and gloom that is following you around. Maybe you have a wave of sadness flow over you. During those times, be careful about trying to find a reason for the emotion. For in seeking to find a reason, you are searching to find someone/something to blame. It is best to simply stand back and process your feelings. It is of no importance why you feel angry/sad/despairing. It doesn't matter who or what might have made you feel that way. Just be aware that you are emotionalizing, and feel the emotion until it dissipates. This will allow you to more easily and effectively move through the soul/mind detox, and will be the first step toward preventing the repetition of patterns. By not focusing on anyone or anything to blame, and by processing the emotion properly, the pattern will run its course and lose its momentum very quickly.

Learning how to be aware of and properly process emotions is part of self-responsibility. Keep in mind we are the sole manufacturer of our outer reality. Taking responsibility is not about blaming someone or yourself. It means to understand that *you are your own creator and your own un-creator*. Sometimes self-responsibility is the harder road to follow, but it offers the greatest rewards.

Proper Way of Dealing with Emotions

In this reality, emotions must be processed. We have already learned how to neutralize the emotional blueprints in Chapters Ten and Eleven. This is essential and needs to be practiced in our calm moments. However, it does not help us when we are completely caught up in an emotional state. Fortunately, the Higher Selves gave us the techniques of how to deal with this, which I'm excited to share with you.

To begin, let's look at emotionalizing from a different perspective. Even though anger and/or grief and/or despair make us feel miserable in some way, these feelings (or any negative emotion) can also be used as a reminder that they need to be addressed. What we can do is shift our viewpoint from, "Everything in my life is falling to pieces. Nothing is working," to, "I am processing an emotion at a very intense level. This is positive for me since now that I have been reminded, I can neutralize these emotional blueprints." Seeing it this way does not mean one just accepts feeling bad. It offers a choice to take action. Emotional blueprints are physically toxic; they cloud our perceptions; they take our focus away from the good in our lives; they lead us to make poor decisions. So now what?

Once reminded, we then want that triggered emotion to process as just that—an emotion. We have already learned how to neutralize emotional blueprints using the Key Exercise. Now let's look at how to handle emotionalizing in the moment it occurs. What we need to learn is how to allow this emotion to be whatever it is at a given point in time. Let's take a look at how to do this.

Exercises

There are three exercises that are important here, and all are simple and straightforward. The first will keep you from blaming others. As was explained in Chapter Five, we are so used to associating the emotion with the event/experience that we lose sight of the fact that the event or the person only triggers the emotional response and is not responsible for that response. So the first exercise helps us learn to disconnect the event and/or person from the emotional response. The other two exercises will give you options for how you may process/neutralize/release an emotion properly in the moment. You can use either or both, depending on what works best for you.

Disconnecting the Event from the Emotion

First, we need to consciously detach our feelings from the event/ person we are blaming. This way, the focus of attention comes back to your emotion. For example, "That jerk just cut me off!" becomes "I'm furious that I've had to slow down!" Don't try this exercise when you are upset because it will be difficult to separate the event/person from the feeling. I recommend that you practice this during a quiet time after the event.

After you have worked with this concept for a while, you will find it easier to pinpoint the emotion/s being triggered in the moment. As a result, you will more quickly identify and properly process your emotions, coming out the other side calm and relieved. By practicing this, you will find yourself blaming people and situations less and less.

To get you started, I will give a few more examples:

> "That bastard screwed me over and put me in an investment that went belly up!" becomes, "I'm mad I made a poor decision about whom I picked as my investment advisor" or "I'm afraid that I won't get by without the money" or "I'm angry that I didn't pay more attention to how my money was being handled."

> "My friend lied to me, pretending to cover my absence with the teacher when I skipped class" becomes, "I am mad that I was caught and have to suffer the punishment."

Pet peeves are good places to start with this exercise as well. For example:

> "The nerve of people who don't respond to my calls/emails" becomes, "I feel ignored and worthless/insignificant when I reach out and don't hear back."
>
> "I refuse to let people who interrupt get away with that rudeness!" becomes, "I get angry when I'm not being listened to."
>
> "Yet again my mother had to make a negative comment about me!" becomes, "I am hurt when seen as lacking in some way."

Proper Release Technique

Now that we are focused on the emotions and not the person/event, I would like to give you an effective technique to use when you are in the thick of emotionalizing. It's very simple and is the same exercise that I was given for my anxiety (which I mentioned in the Author's Preface). This exercise works for every emotion, not just anxiety. For example, something happens, and you are in the throes of anger. Do not blame the trigger. The trigger was created and brought in by your own altered realities. Instead, simply see the anger as black smoke coming out of the top of your head and then turning into white smoke. As long as you feel angry, just keep visualizing the anger's release. Remember it is toxic, and you are simply helping yourself cleanse this toxicity out of your system. You are also not re-empowering your thought forms by blaming someone and obsessing over it. This is a good thing. This is the proper way to process emotions.

I have to be honest. It is often difficult to remember to do this very simple exercise in the moment. The emotions can carry us away, and we may never look back. The good news is that, with practice, it becomes easier and easier. Also, even if you don't do this in the moment, you should do the neutralizing exercises on the Thought Form, Habit, and Emotional Bodies after the fact. Personally, even though I can sometimes be good at releasing while emotionalizing, other times I later realize, that I never even gave the process a second thought. However, I see improvement all the time by keeping up with the Key Exercise. Just do your best.

Working From Inside of the Emotion

You can do this exercise either if you are in the midst of emotionalizing or if you just decide later to work on an emotion that's problematic.

Amalgamate with your Pure Soul Essence, your Higher Selves and become One with the Originating Source. Then project into your Emotional Body simply by thinking it. Ask for and find the emotional blueprint that you want to neutralize. When you locate it, ask to project into the center of this response. You are amalgamated and you are protected. You cannot be touched by the emotional response itself. Once there, see your Pure Soul Essence Light expanding beyond yourself, into the emotion. It is neutralizing the blueprint from the inside out. Just keep expanding the Light until you get a sense that the emotional response is gone or that you have done all you can for the moment.

If you do this exercise while emotionalizing, you need to be sure to amalgamate first. If you have the presence of mind to practice this exercise in the moment in the first place, I am confident you will remember to do so.

I've often said that if I could just come up with a simple solution that helps us remember to process emotions properly every time, I'd be a millionaire. So far it hasn't happened, though I'll never say never. And maybe one of my readers will find that answer. However—again—going back after the fact is invaluable. The Key Exercise works wonders as well. Even if you never remember to properly release during the emotional moments, you will absolutely see more balance, ease and progress with your emotional life from the Key Exercise. Emotions can be difficult, but these exercises will bring you the help you deserve.

Chapter Fourteen: Boxes We Create for Ourselves

Higher Selves Quote

By accepting a belief at any level, you immediately place a boundary around that belief, which limits expansion. So if you hold fast to a belief, you have created a boundary around you that does not permit you to expand beyond that belief. By reaching a point where you are able to stand within the center of belief and disbelief, of accepting neither the truth nor the untruth, you will greatly accelerate and expand your ability to live in an unlimited, nonjudgmental state of beingness.

I once saw a one-panel cartoon of a man standing in front of me, with both his hands holding on to the bars of his jail cell window as he looks out. He is gazing at the beauty of the countryside outside his cell, mournful that he is unable to go out and enjoy nature. What we see that he cannot see is that the other three walls of the jail cell are not there. And we understand, as viewers looking from the outside in, is that all he needs to do is to turn around to be free, that by just changing his viewpoint, he would discover there is no jail cell at all.

This jail cell is symbolic of the boxes we all create for ourselves. They are places we live in by saying such things as, "Oh, I can't do that," "You know me, I'm just that way," "I've tried to do that many times and it's just hopeless," "I'm too afraid/stupid/busy/stressed/upset/whatever to be successful/ happy/good at/better at whatever the current issue is," or even, "I would do that, but my spouse/boss/friend/group would never allow it." There are endless ways that we box ourselves in. Could there be a way for us to find the means and the courage to escape from our boxes and live our life more fully? Yes, of course. Let's look at what is behind the reality of our boxes, understand how we've created them in our lives, and learn to take steps that can free us from out negative perspectives.

Judgments and Beliefs

Judgments—positive or negative—seem to be the cornerstone of the human condition. We all judge throughout our days. We judge ourselves, friends, environment, work, our families, our actions, the weather, the news, or the day's events. Sound familiar? When something is good/positive/at least not painful, we are happy/glad/relieved. When something is bad/unpleasant/hurtful/crazy, we do the best we can with it. However, if you judge something to be correct, whether it is negative or not, then you have created a belief. We all carry beliefs as simple as I'm handsome/plain/ugly or I'm special/decent/challenged. And every time we accept a belief at any level, we create boundaries around ourselves, which act as powerful limitations in our lives.

Beliefs and judgments, therefore, reinforce each other and form symbolic, but very real, prison walls. If you judge yourself as inarticulate, for example, and believe it, you can create a prison that keeps you from speaking out or speaking up. You may shy away from jobs that require verbal ability, either oral or written. You may avoid important discussions with a loved one, feeling it might be a wasted effort. Or you can become someone who overcompensates by explaining the same thing over and over again, hoping that somehow, someone will understand you, when in reality you are boring those who got it the first time.

In other words, judgments and beliefs can rule our lives. They can create self-identities, the characteristics by which we define ourselves—the many boxes that limit us. For example, many of us build our identities around what we do. I am a single mother (and I can't possibly be a good parent all by myself); I am an engineer who works with facts and figures (and can't deal with emotional issues); I am a big talker (and I'm not comfortable in situations where I'm not the center of attention); I'm a professional athlete (and don't need to take time to focus on relationships or ethics); I am a caregiver (and it means I have to sacrifice being cared about). These types of self-identities, (whether completely conscious or not), limit all of us, keeping us in places where we see ourselves as falling short and/or blinding us to other options in life. Finding and breaking down the limitations of our self-identities can empower our efforts to expand and to become more than we currently are.

As an example, let's look at the self-identity of worthlessness. Perhaps you grew up with an extremely stern father who couldn't tolerate imperfection and felt having 100 percent control over you was the answer. When you didn't do what he required and fell short of *his idea* of perfection, he would punish you, making sure you understood what a failure you were. Your feelings of shame and worthlessness dominated your days as you grew up. You internalized his view and began seeing yourself through his eyes, judging yourself as worthless and undeserving on a regular basis. As an adult, you lived in a world of shame at home, at work and in your relationships. Almost every friend abandoned you and left you believing it was your fault, that you were unlovable and worthless as a friend. Clearly, your self-identity of worthlessness has developed to such a great size that it now dominates your life in many arenas.

Past Life Influences

It has been well established in psychology that many of our self-identities are incubated while our parents are raising us. Even in the best of circumstances, where our parents are enlightened and loving, we usually take on their viewpoints about who we are, e.g., "I am the slow but lovable one," "I am the charming trouble-maker," "I am the creative one who has no common sense," "I'm the overachiever who bases self-worth on success in the workplace." This may be how your loving parents saw you, and over time their judgments became your beliefs. Up until today you may think that you have no common sense, aren't creative, are so type-A that your relationships are doomed. Of course, these beliefs could be so much worse if your parents passed on to you pain from their own upbringing, or were seeing you through the lenses of their own deep wounds. No matter the source, self-identities can carry potentially crippling limitations.

What most people may not understand is that the majority of our beliefs have their origins in experiences we couldn't possibly remember from past lives. The projections from these past-life experiences into this lifetime come in the form of our parent thought forms and habits, as you now understand. These thought forms color (or discolor) how our belief systems in this life will be built. But exploring your past lives to get help is not necessary. Just as long as you understand that the basis for your judgments and beliefs are rooted outside of the reality (the life) you are living in now. Hopefully, this information can help free you from the idea that you have to be in the box you're in. If you know that your box/boxes really belong to your minds of the past, maybe it will be easier for you to accept that you can open them up and climb out. It also may help you stop blaming your parents/boss/god/mother nature for whatever you believe you are lacking.

Once again, it is unnecessary to delve into past experiences or past existences in order to unravel the threads that have gone into your current belief system. You carry within yourself—in this life, in this reality—every experience. And you need to go no further than your Thought Form Body to be able to break the boundaries/limitations of your beliefs and judgments. By doing so, you can reach new levels of understanding of who you are, change your perspective on what you can do, and discover a more objective state of beingness.

Standing in the Center of Belief and Disbelief

The Higher Selves have indicated that when a person is presented with information, it is important to not believe what is being told to him/her. By the same token, they also ask that the individual to not disbelieve (in other words, to remain neutral). The goal is to stand in the center of the information presented without making judgments. This sounds so theoretical that it's hard to imagine being able to do it. This is because most of the time we find ourselves in constant movement between believing and disbelieving. But the goal is to accept neither the truth nor the untruth, in order to move out of our limitations and into the deeper layers of who we truly are. To learn how to do this, let's look at the exercise the Higher Selves recommend.

NEUTRALITY EXERCISE

Think of a situation you are in that calls forth one of the beliefs you have about yourself. To help you with this, I will use the example of someone thinking him/herself to be inarticulate. After you read through this, please think of one of your limiting beliefs and then do the exercise again.

Let's imagine that your boss has just asked you (the so-called inarticulate one) to speak tomorrow in front of a group about a project you have worked on and completed. Because you have done a good job, he has asked others outside the department to come in to learn the ropes from you. This brings up your belief that you are unable to communicate clearly, and therefore, you know you will fail. You can't get out of it without quitting your job. What can you do? The steps for the exercise are as follows.

- Find a moment when you have quiet mental space and you won't be interrupted. You begin with the Amalgamation, as we do with every exercise. Focus on the space between belief and disbelief. It is completely neutral. You can imagine the belief on one side of you and the disbelief on the other side. This symbol is only one way to picture it. Use any symbol you are comfortable with, knowing that it is only a symbol but represents a very real place. This is the space I want you to move into. You do so simply by saying, "I am in the neutral space between the beliefs and disbeliefs regarding my ability to communicate." In this space, you will feel neutral about whether or not you're inarticulate. You stand completely free of judgments about yourself. The beliefs are outside of this space and do not touch you here. Spend a few moments experiencing neutrality. If the old voice of the inarticulate belief comes into your mined, refocus on the neutral space.

- Now turn around to see the many different sides of the belief that you are inarticulate. See the criticism of your being inarticulate from new angles. You are now separate from the belief, and no longer held prisoner by it. You may see that there were times in your life when, without thinking, you spoke out easily and effortlessly, and that you were clearly understood the first time. You may see times when others around you didn't understand you because they really weren't listening, or that they were listening, but something inside them made it difficult for them to hear you clearly. You may also come to understand that your message was heard, but only on a subliminal level, so that only later did it become an a-ha moment for the listener. You may also find that some people find you completely easy to understand, but don't speak up to let you know. Or you may find that during your youngest years, the ones who should have been listening to you did not for reasons you may never know. Perhaps this meant that you took on the responsibility for their problem when it really had nothing to do with your communication skills. With these new insights—which your Higher Selves will help you see—you will now be ready to neutralize your old beliefs/disbeliefs.

- Focus on your Pure Soul Essence Light while standing in the center of this neutral space between belief and disbelief. Concentrate on the purity of your Pure Soul Essence in this place, feeling/knowing/sensing your inner beauty and perfection.
- Send your Light out to all the beliefs and judgments that are in the space around this center. Ask that your Light neutralize the belief that you are inarticulate—engulfing all the thought forms, habits and blueprints that have manufactured this belief in this and in past lifetimes.

Similar to the Key Exercise, this approach is yet another way to tackle beliefs that are holding you back. You can also work from this place of neutrality on directly or indirectly related thought forms. Some suggestions would be: people not listening to you, your misunderstandings about what was truly going on, poor self-esteem issues that can easily result in a ripple effect. I would also neutralize fear, anxiety, or any other emotion that could come up when you confront your belief or when you think about the presentation you have to give the next day.

You can also empower with your Light the positive thought form of perfect communication, while, of course, amalgamating it with your Higher Selves. When you are done, you can call in the energies of Divine Love, Divine Mind, Divine Success and Divine Faith in yourself. And now you would be well on your way to moving out of that 'inarticulate' box.

If you were the person in this example, you may still struggle through the presentation in the morning. A strong belief built up over lifetimes may not disappear overnight. You would also need to actually prepare what you are going to say. However, you would notice a shift in some way, like finding out you have more confidence as you go along, or that fewer attendees ask questions about what you said. Or you may get complimented on your presentation, and notice you didn't sweat through your shirt, as you would have before.

This exercise can be done on a daily basis or when you consciously find yourself limited based on a belief. You can also make standing in the center between belief and disbelief a regular part of the Amalgamation. I do that every time now, since it helps me to expand the viewpoint and not to judge myself. If you are in the 'between,' you are in a neutral space, where the perfection of the Pure Soul Essence can more easily penetrate our awareness, because in that space we are not sitting behind veils and clouds of judgments that prevent us from knowing our Light.

Results

Before moving on, it is important to let you know that, in addition to breaking out of your boxes, there are two other very significant results from this work, new perspectives that will begin to permeate your consciousness and create a shift in viewpoint. The first is about your personal choices and the second is about the people that were part of your belief/s.

VIEWPOINT SHIFT ABOUT THE SELF

First, you will understand at deeper and deeper levels that you (using the inarticulate example) have called in all those people who didn't listen, who complained about your being unclear when you spoke, who listened and didn't let you know they heard you, or who were busy and cut you off while you were talking. You will develop (if you haven't already) an acknowledgment and understanding that *these people, situations and conditions could not have been part of your life pattern without your consent* at the thought form level. It is as true here as it was in the chapter on emotionalizing. These people were part of the conditions created within your own Creative Body. The Creative Life Force energy wove your outer reality based on the energy identities you carried, and you continued to create situations where you felt inarticulate. What this means is that we are responsible for what we bring in as our experiences.

Does this mean you need to start blaming yourself for all your issues/patterns/problems? Of course it doesn't. It simply means that you are now going to focus on where you can get the most benefit, that being what you carry within. This is exciting and significant, as this new focus will provide more and more self-motivation to do the exercises in order to continue your movement forward.

VIEWPOINT SHIFT ABOUT OTHER PEOPLE

Do we blame those people in our lives that have created the pattern with us? You know the answer to this already since we covered it in the previous chapter. So no, we don't blame them. Now that we understand our own responsibility, do we ram our new viewpoint down the throats of our co-creators in an attempt to get them to change? Do you think that would help you if the tables were turned? And does it mean that they are off the hook (for being rude/biased/closed off/whatever), since we are now out of our box? No. Everyone is self-responsible on his/her own timing. Then what happens to these other people who were part of our pattern, who fulfilled and empowered the belief that we were inarticulate (or whatever belief we carry)?

Bottom line is that we understand other people have their own boxes and beliefs, just as we do. They were in our lives because their patterns empowered ours, and our patterns empowered theirs. The situations and conditions are co-created. Both/all parties carry the altered realities that created the weaves within the Creative Body, which manifested the beliefs into the physical reality. We magnetically attracted them, and they cooperated perfectly since they harbored the judgments and beliefs that fit with our own. Of course, all parties are, for the most part, unconscious of what was going on underneath. Blaming them helps nothing and only empowers your victim thought form.

Now that you have a deeper understanding of the process, sharing it with someone is perfectly fine and could be very helpful if the other person is open to it. However, you may want to keep in mind that just as you have found your new understanding in your own time, other people will do the same. So, be mindful of their level of interest when sharing. Therefore, allowing them to take responsibility for their own part in the scenario does not let them off the hook. Yet, it is not our responsibility to fix other people, just as it isn't their responsibility to fix us. I suggest that we respect their process and timing while they make their journey, in much the same much the same way that you would want them to respect yours.

Chapter Fifteen: Materialism—The Unexpected Irony

Higher Selves Quote

> *For too long, it has been accepted in general metaphysical and religious circles that the concept of spirituality and the movement along the evolutionary path are done at the expense of the material world in which the individual lives. Yet you are spiritually out of touch when you are materially out of touch, and you are materially out of touch when you are spiritually out of touch.*

One of the most intense issues for so many people involves their finances or lack thereof. It's probable that each and every person who reads this chapter has strong ideas, beliefs, fears, and/or misunderstandings about the material world. Every human soul on this planet is here to work out this balance. Every human chose to be on Earth for the opportunity to break through our false beliefs, misconceptions, fears, limiting truths, and/or self-doubts in order to find expanded understanding and a path toward manifesting equilibrium in our material world.

Why here? The Planet Earth carries a specific energy—that of the Balanced Manifestation of Material Good. All humans who chose to incarnate on Earth are here to unravel the mysteries of the material in their lives, to break through the mental and emotional barriers that keep them from this material balance. Although this book is not meant to impart the details on how the Universe is set up to help souls evolve, the Higher Selves have given us a huge body of information related to just this topic. Despite the chaos and incredible difficulties so many of us have here, there is actually great order in the Universe, even if we cannot see it. In fact, there is tremendous help provided for all souls throughout the Human Kingdom. The example provided here (which is only a small part of the help we receive) relates to planets.

In the Universe, there are an infinite number of solar systems comparable to our solar system. The planets in all solar systems inhabited by evolving life forms carry specific energies that are utilized by the souls on those planets. (The role of the planet is fully explained in my next book on the Universe.) Our planet carries the energy of Proper Material Balance. Just being on this planet means that at the soul level we are committed to learning, understanding, manifesting, and using material good in the Highest Ideal.

That may sound like something out of science fiction, but doesn't it make sense? Material and financial issues abound throughout the human population, no matter what country or area of the world. These issues are the cause of so much of the planet's struggle, from wars to business and from health to relationships. Clearly, most of us have a long way to go to reach successful self-understanding and balance in this area.

Common Viewpoints/Misconceptions

Although I am generalizing, many of us would view being materialistic as a negative thing. We almost automatically put the rich into the category of being greedy, snobbish, or out-of-our-league. When we actually meet someone who is rich and a wonderful person, don't we say something like, "He's rich, but not like what you would think he'd be. He is nice and so down-to-earth." We have to show that this person is, in some way, an exception to the rule. Don't we also assume that everyone rich is happy, and that if only we could be rich, we'd be happy too?

On the other side of the coin, we unconsciously put someone who has devoted their lives to the spiritual realm, such as a Tibetan monk or Mother Teresa, onto the highest pedestal. We may feel that we are too selfish and would never measure up to their high standard of spirituality. If we still have extra money in the bank or a little extra time on the weekends, but are not serving at a soup kitchen or donating every extra dime, we assume we're following short in comparison.

These beliefs and judgments are holding us prisoner. In fact, a material focus is not synonymous with greed, and a spiritual focus is not synonymous with self-sacrifice. The judgment that materialism is a negative thing (because we connect it to greed and callousness) can hold us back from finding our true material good. If we somehow get a chance to fly first class, eat at an expensive restaurant or buy a Gucci handbag, we may apologize and assure people we haven't been sucked into thinking we're privileged. And we portray it as just a one-time thing because somehow it makes us feel less guilty about having some luxury in our lives? Or maybe we feel superior because we have a luxury our friends don't. Either way, there are distortions and limitations around the balance of the material and the spiritual.

Many people are struggling to earn a living and are also trying to do at least some small things to benefit others, though we most likely don't feel successful in either area.

Materialism

So what does it mean to be materialistic? Does it mean that we are greedy and focused on hoarding and accumulating money? Does it mean we have to step on others to be successful? Those are a couple of the connotations and judgments we project on to the word materialism. Yet we have another way to look at this.

The highest level of the meaning of materialism is simply to take something from the abstract and to make it concrete—to materialize something into our physical reality. Finding the significance and balance of material good, learning how to materialize properly in life, is what all of us are here on the planet to learn.

Materializing into the concrete is not only about money; it is also about the manifestation of anything into a material form. The material balance also includes the development and understanding of how to properly use whatever we have materialized. We all have materialized a physical body. Do we have a healthy body? How are we treating ourselves? We all have gifts and talents. How are we doing on manifesting and using them? Money is only one part of our material good; yet for most of us, it is the area that feels most important relative to everything else. So this is the area I am addressing in this chapter. I bring these other elements to you so you can think about them and be aware of them. The energy on planet Earth helps all areas of balanced materializing and proper use of the physical form.

The basic idea is that a balanced material world is essential to your physical reality. By standing in the center between belief and disbelief of the biases we may have against materialism, we will better understand that materialism is an essential part of the human equation and is as important as the spiritual. No matter how spiritual you may be, with few exceptions you still have to pay the rent, put food in your mouth, and operate in the society at large. Clearly, it isn't feasible for the entire human population to move into ashrams, monasteries or communes in order to be spiritual. So that means we each need to find the balance within the lives we are living now.

The Unexpected Irony

This brings me to the very unexpected irony of life. The very thing that you would not expect to help you become more spiritual is the very thing that will help: being more material. This is ironic only because of our misunderstandings and negative biases toward abundance in the material world.

If your focus enables you to bring in material abundance, then you have space and resources to focus on an abundant spiritual life. To be healthy at the spiritual level is to be able to continue your focus of attention on your spiritual goals. To do so, you must have the material balance taken care of. If you are hungry, you cannot focus your attention on the spiritual. You must focus your attention on your growling belly. The balance, therefore, will be off-kilter. If there is lack in your life—any lack of manifestation in your life's circumstances that makes you unhappy—it causes you to focus on that lack, that discomfort or that dissatisfaction. *And that is not spiritual.* Therefore, focusing on the material balance in your life, bringing it into a state of abundance and harmony will allow you to more consistently and productively focus on the spiritual side of life.

Pitfalls

What stands in the way of our material good?

- **Beliefs and Judgments**: Because money, finances and materialism are such highly charged and misunderstood topics, it is important to look at our beliefs surrounding them. Many are likely to be deeply buried in our subconscious. This is why financial good can be an area we consistently work on but end up frustrated by, due to minimal results. When this happens it is a sure bet that we are still in possession of very real and potentially negative beliefs relating to money. In fact, you need to look no further than your own present life. On the surface, almost everyone wants to have financial security, but underneath, unconscious beliefs can sabotage our efforts. Have you ever apologized for riding in a limo or getting orchestra seats to an event? Is it out of a sense of guilt that we had a luxury someone else didn't have? Is it because we pride ourselves on being a "man of the people," and this ticket didn't fit our image of ourselves? Or is it that we believe we don't deserve any better in our lives?

Let me give you an example of one hidden (unconscious) belief. I have a friend, a parent with several children, who was living in debt years ago, wondering from where the next meal for her family would come. Then one summer, long ago, we were both doing the neutralizing and empowering work to improve our finances. After doing the exercises with her a few times, I realized that even though my friend said consciously and often that she wanted more money, and even though she worked hard to neutralize all her poverty thought forms, once in a while I would hear an aside from her, almost a throwaway line, that had an extremely negative bias toward the wealthy. It seemed completely out of place next to her great desire to bring in money, so at first we almost missed it. When we finally became aware of it, we did some digging.

It turned out that my friend hadn't been happy growing up in her wealthy family and from early childhood had equated her father's hard, unfeeling attitude with his obsession with money. This childhood misunderstanding had given birth to the belief (or at least reinforced what she had brought in from other lifetimes) that she would become like her father—narrow-minded and heartless—if she ever had money. She hadn't understood that her father most likely would have been heartless even if poor. Therefore, this powerful belief held her prisoner in a state of poverty and had to be addressed. Fortunately, once she did so, her life turned around, and she found a well-paying job that paid off her debt and gave her the financial security she was looking for and still does to this day.

All judgments, conscious or unconscious, are part of our Thought Form Body, working to weave situations that keep us poor, jobless and/or living paycheck to paycheck.

- **Stealing**: There is a second pitfall that may be less obvious, one that has to do with stealing. Of course we understand that stealing is a crime and is not an ethical thing to do. I'm sure almost everyone doesn't think this is something that applies to him or herself. And I certainly don't think of all of humanity as thieves—not at all; but let me assure you that this issue is important.

  How many of us rationalize exaggerating on an insurance claim to get more money back? Maybe we have fudged on our taxes to get a larger refund? How about not mentioning to a cashier when he/she makes a mistake and forgets to charge us for one of our items? Perhaps, occasionally we have thought to ourselves, "I'll just take the towels/ashtrays from the hotel room. They won't be missed, but I could use them." I would guess that most of us have rationalized like this at least once in awhile. We might feel that it isn't really 'taking' because in our minds it's okay—these are large establishments that make lots of money, right?

  Thinking this way doesn't mean we will be damned or that we are unforgivable. Instead, this type of rationalization has a powerful consequence, of which we may be unaware. I'm not mentioning this to be rigid, self-righteous or judgmental. My reason for bringing this up is because this misunderstood scenario is a significant way we keep ourselves from bringing in the material abundance we deserve, and because, for the most part, this concept is not well understood. When we take in this manner, without giving something in return (money, services, goods), we reinforce and grow within, the subtle but very real belief that *we cannot afford it*. This belief is a major factor in holding us in a state of lack, and we clearly don't want anything to hold us back from our material good.

How to Bring in the Balance?

The bottom line is that if our spiritual goals are set to such a degree that everything else falls by the wayside, it's just as detrimental to us as for people who only set up materialistic goals and ignore their spiritual side. Everyone has a right to a meaningful and balanced life. The lack of material abundance also means that there is a lack of spiritual abundance and vice versa. Just as the word material is not synonymous with greed, the word spiritual should not be synonymous with self-sacrifice. Equilibrium is the goal for all humanity and is especially the focus of attention for souls on this planet (and all planets within the Human Kingdom Universe that carry this same energy).

You have already learned the Key Exercise, and I hope you are already working on the financial lack/abundance energy identities previously discussed in the book (Chapter Ten). And you can also work on any beliefs and judgments you find lurking around in your thoughts by standing in the center of neutrality. Are you one who believes you cannot be spiritual if you have any material abundance? Are you one who believes self-sacrifice is the only way to find spiritual fulfillment? Do you immediately feel that great wealth is out of the realm of possibility for you? Or that if someone has great wealth there is no hope for great spirituality since money corrupts? Do you feel that money might make you a target in some way? Please ask yourself where your beliefs lie. And as you uncover them, work to neutralize them. They are only blinders that limit you, that keep the world of abundance from your doors and keep you in a state of 'the have not.' Thankfully, the Earth carries powerful energy that we can use to our great advantage once we understand how.

The Pure Soul Essence of Earth

The planetary energy that Earth carries is held within Earth's Pure Soul Essence. Yes, Earth, being part of the Mineral Kingdom, also carries a Pure Soul Essence. The planet is as much a part of the Originating Source as is Humanity or any other level of beingness. Perhaps, it is a bit bizarre to think in those terms and may upset some (who cannot fathom a rock as having a soul), though that is not my intention.

At one level, the planetary systems may be viewed as being at the opposite ends of the pole from Originating Source. As I'll be explaining further in Chapter Eighteen, Originating Source de-intensified its energy, resulting in the manifestation of itself as the solar systems, the densest materialization of Originating Source's physical form. As do all parts of Originating Source, these solar systems carry the perfection of their parent—the Pure Soul Essence. Though Originating Source runs at such a high rate of speed that it virtually seems to be standing still, the planetary systems (the Mineral Kingdoms) run at such a low rate of speed that they, also, seem to be virtually standing still. They are polar opposites but are truly the same, though in different form.

Therefore, the Pure Soul Essence of Earth carries the perfection and neutrality of the Originating Source, with Divine Material Balance being its specific empowered energy. Thus, we will greatly assist ourselves by bringing Divine Material Balance into our own lives by learning to utilize this powerful energy. Keeping in mind that our Thought Form Bodies are in a state of great imbalance—the negative so much more pervasive than the positive—the Divine Material Balance that the Earth provides will speed up the manifestation of the proper material good in our lives. Let's take a look at how we can use it.

Exercise

To begin, I ask that each of you commit to your materialistic health and accept it. Money is only energy—a vital energy. Every individual is the rightful owner of as much materialistic good as he/she is willing to accept and commit to. Its proper use (the other essential element to Divine Material Balance) will enable us to be spiritual as well. A commonly held belief on this planet is that to be spiritual, one has to be unselfish to the point where giving involves a tremendous amount of self-sacrifice. However, if one is off balance after having offered others so much of his/her own material good, the proper use of Divine Material Balance is still misunderstood.

To help us all bring in the proper manifestation, understanding, and use of Divine Material Balance, I will give you an exercise that utilizes Earth's very powerful and pure energy.

- As is customary, please do the Amalgamation with your Pure Soul Essence, your Higher Selves and the Originating Source. This is essential to protect yourself from any possible negative energy surrounding the planet. Once you are amalgamated, I ask that you say, "I project into the Pure Soul Essence of the Planet Earth." It is just that simple. Sit for a few moments and just experience the energy. It may seem weird to be projecting into something solid at first. At least I remember thinking that. Of course you aren't moving your body into the Earth, only your consciousness. Just as you would imagine being on a beach or watching a sunset, you would do this the same way. For me, I don't 'see' anything, and I don't even know exactly where the Earth's Pure Soul Essence is. But as my Pure Soul Essence is clearly within me, I imagine Earth's is also within. Once there, you may find that there is a nurturing quality to the energy, bringing you a sense of peace and tranquility. Just enjoy and experience it.

- Once you have accustomed yourself to this energy, say to yourself all that you want to materialize in your life, using "I have" in all statements. Unlike mantras or positive thoughts that simply empower the thought forms, these "I have" statements actually activate the Balanced Energy of Manifestation into your life because you are in the Pure Soul Essence of the Earth. I've written a few out just for some examples: "I have financial abundance. I have a rewarding job. I have a meaningful relationship. I have a perfect place to live. I have the child I want. I have proper love for myself. I have perfect health." Use this type of statement for almost anything. You can see it isn't just about money. It is about materializing balance in all areas of life, including, but not limited to, finances. With these statements, while you are amalgamated and held within the Earth's Pure Soul Essence, *you are triggering this powerful planetary energy that will only work in your Highest Ideal.* Because our souls chose to be on this planet, the understanding and manifestation of the Divine Material Balance is the most significant concept we have to learn about and utilize properly. And we can do it.

In case you're wondering if using the Earth's energy to help your material life can also empower the negatives in your life, I would like to be clear. Absolutely not. The energy is operating on the Divine frequency level and can only work in one's Highest Ideal.

It brings in balance to one's patterns, as it is working from the Pure Soul Essence, with the same Light we use to neutralize our altered realities. Finally, I would like to point out that bringing in material abundance is not synonymous with abusing Earth's resources or other people to accomplish the task. The proper acquisition and use of the material is an equal part of the Balance of Material Good. The energy cannot be used as an aid to manipulate others for devious reasons.

Results

From an everyday perspective, some of us may feel guilty, afraid, undeserving or unable to accept comfort into our lives. Yet it is our right, our privilege and even our responsibility to enjoy material balance. It allows us to bring in spiritual balance. By working with the Earth's vital energy, along with doing the Key Exercise, the important balance in life will manifest for all of us. Now, whenever I do the Amalgamation, I also project into the Pure Soul Essence of Earth to get the additional help to manifest whatever I am working on. I suggest you do the same, since it is as simple as adding the statement, "I also project into the Pure Soul Essence of Earth" at the end of the three statements of Amalgamation. You do not need to say the "I haves" each time though I encourage you to do so.

There is no predetermined level of material wealth, since each person will find his/her own pathway. Some might be exponentially wealthy, with the ability to set up foundations and donate money and resources to good causes. Others might simply have enough to live a modest life but find smaller ways to give back, such as working as a Big Brother, helping with animal rescues, befriending a soldier overseas, or donating blood on a regular basis. There is also no one right way to be spiritual. Some people may feel moved to go to Calcutta (or elsewhere) to help serve the poor, while some will stay home to help in their own neighborhood. Some may be able to help the masses, and others will help one or a few. All ways are valid and all ways are significant. Each individual will manifest the balance differently. It is important not to compare yourself to anyone else. The balance is there for everyone to attain in his/her own unique way.

Chapter Sixteen: Chaos

Higher Selves Quote

Chaos is the energy of transformation. It transforms the old order into the new order, which is always a higher, more positive order. Yet the process of chaos and change often creates for us, as individuals, tremendous conflict. Chaos, within its center, is extremely neutral, but because we are unable to enter into the center of chaos properly, we become the chaos, and by becoming the chaos, we create the conflict in our outer reality.

We have all experienced the trials and tribulations of chaos in our lives. The chaos could stem from a natural disaster, an unexpected death of a loved one, an extreme financial loss or an illness that completely changes your life. And these are only a few of the hundreds of scenarios that can throw us into complete chaos, taking over our lives for days, weeks, months or even years. Like emotionalizing, chaos can catch us up in its whirlwind so that we focus our attention on the problems, spinning us out of control. We see chaos as the stuff of nightmares. We know our lives will never be the same, we feel powerless to stop it and we dread the outcome.

What if it doesn't have to be like that? Could there be another way to look at situations and conditions even if it seems that nothing good could come them? Let's take a closer look at our assumptions and see what the Higher Selves have to say about chaos.

What Is Chaos?

Chaos could be viewed as the natural order (or disorder, depending on which side of chaos you happen to be viewing at any point in time) of the Universe. It is a state of existence within which every living soul must dwell at different points in his/her life's journey. It is not created to test or to punish. Instead, it is a *transformational* energy, the force that moves us from the old to the new. In other words, it is the powerful energy that creates change in our lives.

When describing the very real energy of chaos, the Higher Selves used words that may surprise you. They explained that the energy of chaos (change) is one that is quiet, calm and tranquil. The symbolic picture they gave of it was a giant ball of energy that is in a continuous state of fluctuation and motion. Yet, the essence of this fluctuating energy is the state of complete balance and harmony. There are no negative energies here. This is chaos in its truest form.

How It Affects Us

Chaos literally is the movement that carries us from the dissolution of the old form to the creation of a new form. This covers any change, seemingly positive or negative.

A simple example is a pregnant mother before giving birth. She is in a state of the 'old order', being pregnant. The energy of chaos activates, and through the chaotic patterns of movement within that mother's system, the child is born and a 'new order' is created. In other words, the mother is no longer pregnant, and the child is no longer a part of the mother. By using the example of childbirth, we can see that change does not always mean something negative. Of course, we don't call childbirth chaos.

We only call it chaos when the change is perceived as negative, though the energy involved is identical.

What often happens is that we view change as chaos when we are in conflict with the loss of the old as it gives birth to the new. We don't see a conflict when a child is born, since we would not want the old order—the state of pregnancy—to continue. Instead, we welcome childbirth. However, there are many instances where it is difficult to accept the loss of the old order. We don't want to move, lose friends, a marriage, a loved one, our health, or to be in the center of a natural disaster, a train crash or a car pile-up. If, as the change manifests in our lives, we are happy/comfortable/at ease with the old way, and the new order seems forced upon us, it can be terrifying or frightening because of the unknown road ahead.

Therefore, at the first sign of trouble, we dive into the fray, fighting blindly to hold on while finding our lives at least temporarily out of our control. There is no time to think; our brains shut down; we become focused on one thing, that of doing everything in our power to fight against the energy (the change). Often, no sooner do we get through one thing when something else comes in from another direction. We stand in the energy field and often, all we can think of is, "Just get me out of this!" Or "When am I going to wake up and find out it is all just a dream?" And so it goes. Truly, this is what we experience as chaos.

Taking the Victim Out of Chaos

Chaos (change) has now arrived in our lives in whatever form it takes for each of us. Let me remind you that nothing can happen to us that, at the soul level, we don't permit to happen. In fact, we have been the creators of the change in our lives as we are the master weavers from within our own Creative Body. So when we are brought into a situation where chaotic energies exist, each of us has agreed to be there. Any condition that we find ourselves involved in, as far as chaos is concerned, is a place where we belong, for we have made that choice. This may not feel good to you (perhaps because it can be easier to blame someone or something), but understanding this is the first place to start.

The other essential part of this is that the new order comes in at a higher frequency, a higher level of existence. Chaos is a Divine Energy. It cannot trespass free will, so if we are in it it's because we have called it in. We are ready at the soul level to move forward, and it is not because we are bored or just curious. In fact, this is the way of the soul's evolution. It is part of the Divine journey for us all. (Much more on soul evolution is in the next book on the Universe.) But it often means that things/people are being removed from our lives that we don't want to see go or new things are introduced that we seem sure won't be good. We may not want to say goodbye to the ones leaving us or have to start over with a new place to live. We want the status quo. That's where we're comfortable. It's what we know. Change can be hard because we have no idea what the future will be.

You are going through this erosion process so that you can rebuild (with the chaos energy) something better. You are creating new beginnings. Moving forward can be scary, overwhelming, painful and/or confusing, depending on the form it takes. However, you are the master of your own destiny, not a puppet being manipulated by someone/something/Mother Nature. Change is inevitable. It is the natural state of existence.

It's also important to not interpret the chaos in your life as evidence that you are psychologically wounded/a wacko/off your rocker or that you are a failure/ignorant/unlucky. To judge yourself or others here (as you will remember) holds you prisoner to negative beliefs.

Also, we don't have to be a part of the outer chaotic conditions. We have another way to deal with its effect. I will show you how to experience the serenity and calm within chaos energy that is constantly in motion.

Finding Order and Tranquility

The Thought Form Body, Habit Body, and the Emotional Body are the three interlocking etheric frequencies that are the engines that run your life, manifest the chaos and weave the totality of your life pattern. What do we do then when something occurs to us or to a loved one that brings chaos into the mix?

First, use the Key Exercise on the energy identities that are part of the situation you are experiencing. Properly processing the emotional responses becomes essential here. As often as you can remember to do it, let the emotional responses such as panic, confusion, fear, guilt, blame, despair, misery, etc., move out through the top of your head, imagining it as black smoke turning white. This will help tremendously. If remembering to do that is elusive, please do the Key Exercise when you have the mental space for it, and work on the specific chaotic situation, whether it be a betrayal by a spouse, the loss of a home, an unwelcome career change or a life-threatening illness. The soul is using these situations, brought in by altered realities, to bring about your life's transformation. Even though any one of these things can seem so overwhelming that you feel you are trying to hold back a tidal wave with a toothpick, finding even a few minutes to do the Key Exercise—whether it be in the shower, while unloading the dishwasher or waiting in the hospital waiting room—will be immensely beneficial.

Additionally, it is important to get used to the idea that chaos is the platform upon which the new order is built after the old order has been destroyed. The energy behind it, the energy of chaos, carries the tranquility and balance we want, need and have access to, even though it is always in a state of flux. If we can connect with that beautiful energy and take ourselves out of the frenzy, the panic and the knee-jerk reactions, we can find the peace and order to get through the chaos. We can slow it down, move out of the whirlwind and find clarity within. This way, we would be *in* chaos but not *of it*. We can learn how to live peaceful, calm, tranquil and balanced lives while chaos takes place all around us. We can find the solutions to problems more easily and more accurately, helping ourselves and assisting others as well. Let's find out how.

Exercise

Before we begin this exercise, please amalgamate by saying, "I am the Light of my Pure Soul Essence, as it expands in through and around my physical body and my etheric bodies. I project into the Originating Source, and in this state of connection at the highest level, I am amalgamated with the Totality of my Higher Selves." The Amalgamation is always important, and in the first part of this particular exercise, the Higher Selves will place a shield of energy around you.

- What I want you to do is take a moment to focus on the chaos in your life right now. If you are currently in a state of balance, think about the chaos you have experienced in the past year. We are going to begin by experiencing chaos as we normally do—standing right in the center of it, blasted from all sides. I want you to think about the chaotic situation and allow yourself to be in the chaos. Please let in anything that has upset you, freaked you out or created schisms in your energy field. Feel that energy swirl around you, hitting you from top to bottom. Feel yourself caught up in it. You are 'kaleidoscoping.' Feel it, but don't be alarmed. You're not taking any of this into the Thought Form Body, since the Higher Selves are protecting you with a shield. So just let it all hang out.

- Now, by thinking or imagining it, you just sloooowwww doooowwwwn the energy. You slow it down. Watch it, as you take the whirlwind out of the swirl. You can envision the slowing as if you've created the eye of the hurricane. You don't have to slow down all the energy. You only have to create your place of calm in the center. Find the calm, find the balance, find the serenity and be completely at peace, completely harmonized while all of that chaotic energy moves around you. Chaos cannot touch you. You may feel it in an external way, but within this center you are calm and peaceful and tranquil. And because you are standing where the energy is so slow that it feels motionless, you are able to understand and anticipate the positive, higher levels of change that are being brought to you by the movement from the old to the new. Connect with the Higher Selves. Connect with your Pure Soul Essence. Feel them as they assist you in finding and supporting order in your life. You can see what is occurring with new eyes. Now that you have left the blinding storm of the chaos itself, you will find the clarity of vision that will help lift your perspective from one of hopelessness to one of proper action and focus. This place of calm is always yours to claim.

From now on, when doing this exercise, it's not necessary to stand in the center of chaos again, since I am guessing you are already in it if you are reusing the exercise. I ran it this way so you could experience the feeling of chaos as it usually manifests, as opposed to the serenity of true chaos, the energy of tranquility. From now on, when life is in complete disarray, find that place, that eye of the hurricane you have already created and experienced, where the energy has slowed down to stillness. I encourage you to use this exercise any time life throws you completely off balance, when you become part of a situation or condition that results in change. I understand that practice make perfect. Even if you only remember to use it once in a while, it will go a long way in helping you move through any transformational phase.

Instead of allowing change to control you so you can't focus on anything except fighting, resisting or putting up walls for protection from the energies as they slam you around, you now have a technique to slow the onrush down, to help you center yourself in the calm of the storm. Change is inevitable. We can fight it, or we can change our viewpoints about it and use the energy provided.

Viewpoint—the Key to Helping Yourself

Again, chaos is the natural state of transformation, yet it is also the negatively charged word we use to describe the effects of change. You now know that change is actually a neutral event (sound familiar?). Our perspective on it determines whether we see it as positive or negative and whether we move through it easily or with great difficulty. So chaos for one individual may not be chaos for another. Why? It is the viewpoint and the projection of that viewpoint that makes the difference. If negative, the viewpoint creates a conflict that results in chaos for that individual. Having a baby, for example, can bring great joy and serenity to the mother, but it could throw a father into a state of chaos if he were unaware of the pregnancy.

Let's look at another example. When betrayed by a cheating spouse, one could react in an extremely negative way, leading to months filled with anger and resentment that leads to the obsession with the idea of getting revenge on the wayward lover. We all might understand this reaction and feel even in some cases feel it to be completely justified. Yet this type of response has a way of attaching the betrayed spouse to chaotic energies and makes the subsequent separation and divorce messy, bitter, drawn out, and extremely expensive. Another person in the same situation may see it differently. Instead of being angry, he/she may be relieved since the marriage could have been loveless for a long time. Even though he/she knows that it would have been easier to stay with the status quo of living together, he/she may understand that there would also be downsides to this arrangement. No real joy. No happiness. No sharing. No intimacy. No movement. Yes, even this perspective would involve the upheaval of change in one's daily life. But if one realizes that the stagnation in the marriage was actually unbearable, the transition through the change would be easier, as the focus would be on the steps needed to separate their lives and not tied up in emotionalizing. Perhaps this viewpoint is just what it takes to make the divorce less contentious, less expensive and less time-consuming. Focusing on the practical brings flexibility to the table and allows one to be in chaos without being caught up in it.

Just to be clear, there is also a chance that the betrayal could trigger deeper understanding in both parties about the communication problems in the marriage. If there is a realization that the event was co-created, it's possible that both spouses could see the betrayal as a symptom of a marriage that's off track. Rather than get a divorce, the couple might focus on the connection problems, find new priorities and heal the areas in the marriage that were at the root of the betrayal. It may not be easy. It would mean a good deal of self-introspection and facing the internal pain that fueled the original problems. Yet, there is much hope especially with all the tools presented in *CHOICES*.

In summary, change can be hard no matter the viewpoint and circumstances. When great problems come into your life, I suggest that you ignore the negative connotations of the word 'chaos' and focus instead on the word 'change'. For help with this, amalgamate and stand in the center of the stillness and tranquility of the chaos energy. This energy will help you understand that it is the natural order of things, something that you co-created with all others around you. You can now move inside it to find that serenity, balance and order. Slow down the spinning. Practice with it whenever you are feeling overwhelmed or at a loss for what to do. Amalgamate and become aware of your Pure Soul Essence, that purest point of personal power. Find the calm in the storm.

The Stark Truth

By now, most of you may be thinking about a tragedy, or some kind of change that, no matter how hard you try, you've never been able to see any good come of it. You cannot understand why your wife died or your best friend became paralyzed. And I would like to address this as best I can in this book. If we knew at the conscious level the ins and outs of our soul's journey, everything would make sense to us. (More on a soul's journey to come in a future book.)

However, this is not meant to be an excuse. This is not the same as saying that the death was God's will, that He works in mysterious ways, and that we just have to accept it. Instead, this is bringing the focus back to the fact that the change, whatever it is, is not imposed upon us by another force such as God, fate or bad luck. We live in the Free Will Kingdom and are creating our outer reality on a moment-to-moment basis based on the beliefs and judgments carried at the thought form level. If we were completely conscious and stood within the whole of our soul's journey, we would clearly understand why change happened. Because we're not there, it can be more difficult to understand and accept.

What's important to grasp (as best you can) is that if we have manifested something extremely difficult in our lives, there's something positive that will be gained from it. We've attracted this situation to ourselves so we can move on to new levels of awareness and experience. There is something to learn. There is something to be gained. The chaotic/perhaps earth-shattering event has occurred in our lives because we are ready, at some level, to move forward. Also, we're now aware that there are altered realities lurking in our etheric bodies. It's the chance we have provided ourselves to discover deep patterns we no longer want. It brings us closer to knowing what thought forms, emotional blueprints and habits we need to neutralize, and that can be a powerful motivator!

As we neutralize our patterns and blinders (which have called in the chaos), we can learn new perspectives, develop ourselves in ways we never thought, experience more meaningful relationships and become more properly self-connected and self-aware. We may even become role models for others through inspiration and leadership. Therefore, I would encourage you to work with the exercises provided. Neutralize all the energy identities that you can think of and whenever you are in chaos, find your place in the center of the calm, where the energy is motionless and serene.

Finding our way out of misery can be difficult. I have certainly experienced that myself. So I promise you that I am not saying, "Just get over it." That type of response helps no one and doesn't give the person who is suffering the respect and caring he/she needs. In our own time, we all have our own ways of processing the resolution of our problems. What we *can* offer one another is caring, respect and effective tools to help. Each of us is responsible for our own movement forward, and supporting one another in the journey is invaluable. The next two chapters in Part IV are there to provide great comfort and solace for those difficult and seemingly unsurpassable times. They also help make the good times even better.

Part 4

THE HEART OF THE MATTER

Chapter Seventeen: Your Pure Soul Essence

Higher Selves Quote

You are all—every single individual in this room and every single individual on this planet or any other planet—beautiful, perfect, wonderful, marvelous and all-powerful. It is through unconsciousness that you do not recognize this. You wear the Thought Form Body like dark glasses, and because you've never taken them off, you don't know that the world is a brighter and more beautiful place. As you cultivate this inner perfection, and reach the state of emotionally feeling that perfection, everything around you becomes perfect. When you are functioning out of that Pure Soul Essence, that spark that is part of the totality of Originating Source, you are living the very highest, most perfect existence that is possible.

Remember the game of Clue? It involves players competing to solve the murder mystery of who did it (Colonel Mustard?), in what room (the Conservatory?) and with what weapon (the candlestick?). The game board depicts a two-dimensional house with a layout of its various rooms. There are several ways to get into and out of each room. There are doors, underground passages, long hallways and even shortcuts that give you faster access when moving through the house. Now imagine the house in Clue as a symbol of your life, with its many rooms pertaining to the various parts of your existence—the love room, health room, finance room, destiny room, relationship room, etc. Of course, there would be many more rooms than in most houses, and some of them would overlap, such as a living room that also includes a dining area. It's not necessary to draw a map here or fill in any details of your house. I only ask that you keep that simple picture in mind.

In Clue, the purpose of the board is not solely to travel between rooms for the fun of it, but to reach a goal: to solve the murder mystery. Perhaps, like Clue, there is a goal or purpose to our lives behind all that movement throughout our rooms. In Clue, you visit each room to get the clues needed to solve the case, but in life, what purpose would there be? Most of us work the rooms to handle life as best we can. We learn and grow from spending time in these rooms, gaining insights, wisdom and tools to help us on our life's journey. We raise children, have careers, try to help the less fortunate and may follow some type of spiritual path. However, there are so many complexities, misconceptions, fears, hurts and problems in life that often we have to find better ways to handle all that our rooms contain. Of course, there are also people who accept the cards they are dealt, good or bad, without question.

For many of us, one of our main goals is happiness. If nothing else, we want to be happy and fulfilled in our lives. That is an honest, worthy and valid goal. If we look at humanity at large, we find that happiness is experienced along a continuum, from miserable to ecstatic. Each individual finds his/her place on that line. Three questions come to mind at this point: Is happiness all there is? Is there a good/better way to find it? Could there be yet another goal?

In order to answer these questions, I am going to present another way of looking at our goals, a different way to think about the rooms in our house (our life). What if there was a room we were never aware of, a secret, hidden room? What if just finding out that a hidden room exists was part of the goal of life? What if all the other rooms in the house were there so we could discover the hidden room? Where is this room? What's inside of it? What does it mean for each of us? How can we use it? These are important questions that need to be answered. Let's begin.

Is There a Secret Room?

Of course, you must have guessed that I wouldn't have asked this question if there weren't one. So yes, there is a room that is vastly important to all of us in our lives. All of humanity is on a journey to discover this room, to experience it and to be it. It holds all that we are and all that we will be. So where is this hidden room?

Where Is the Hidden Room?

You may think that if only you could search long enough and be smart enough you would find the route to this hidden treasure. You may believe, for example, that if you spend more time in the spirituality room than in the financial room, you might find the necessary clues. Or perhaps you may feel that by spending all your time in the family room and almost none in the personal interest room you are on your way to finding your purpose in life.

However, it turns out that the room is not hidden under, over or within one of the other rooms. And it is not about the amount of time you spend in one room as opposed to another. *Instead, the room has been inside you all along*. You bring it to every area in the house of life each and every time you move around, whether you are in the family room, career room or health room. You are carrying this hidden treasure, not in your hands, but in your soul. When this room is discovered, opened up, understood, and utilized, it provides power, expanded understanding, and an astonishing increase in the good in your life.

What Is Inside This Room?

The title of this chapter, of course, gives you the answer to this question. However, I must state it again. The hidden room contains our Pure Soul Essence. I have introduced the concept of the Pure Soul Essence briefly in earlier chapters, and hopefully it's become a regular part of your Amalgamation. However, it's time to expand your understanding of this treasure. This knowledge will provide the energy and know-how that will enable you to upgrade all of life's other rooms. It will help you beautify your life's 'décor' and bring more joy and meaning to your journey.

What Is the Pure Soul Essence?

The Pure Soul Essence is part of the actual Soul of Originating Source. This means that every soul in the Universe contains within it the essence/a spark of the Creator of All There Is. The Higher Selves use the term *Soul Aspect* to describe this part of Originating Source. When Originating Source began the manifestation of the Universe, it sent parts of itself (aspects) out into the Universe, de-intensifying the energy until it manifested and created the world (the galaxies, stars, and planets) as we know and see it. Everything we see in the material world contains an aspect of Originating Source, a piece of its soul. These aspects are what we call the Pure Soul Essence. (The long explanation of this process will be included in the next book on the Universe.)

A way to understand this is to look at what happens to our DNA when we procreate. When we give birth, our offspring contain the DNA from both parents; this part of ourselves is carried within our children. The Aspects of the Originating Source work in much the same way. With our DNA, our children get half from each parent; then their children get half, so that the DNA from one parent becomes diluted in future generations as the DNA from others is added. When the Originating Source distributes aspects of itself to each and every soul, however, there is no watering-down effect. The Pure Soul Essence contains all that the Originating Source was, is, and is becoming. Every soul's Pure Soul Essence is whole and perfect in every way.

The connection between the aspects and their source is constant and can never be lost or stolen. The journey for each of us is to become conscious of our inner purity and to connect with that knowledge on the feeling level, knowing in every sense of the word that we are one with the Originating Source.

What Is the Shocking and Brilliant Significance of This?

The meaning for each and every one of us is that *we are* not *flawed. We are perfect.* How can that be?

We are the perfection of our Pure Soul Essence. This is the true essence of every living being in the Universe. The journey of every being is to move from the Mineral Kingdom into higher and higher levels of awareness. At the Human Level, our consciousness is able to reach this point of understanding. It's the beginning of the end goal of our journey in the Human Kingdom. Until we get there, it's as if the Pure Soul Essence is asleep. It's time for us to wake it up! Therefore, the first step on this journey is simply to become aware of our purity and perfection, even if we don't fully understand it.

I can understand your possible skepticism since we so often see imperfections in the world. We judge others and ourselves as lacking in many ways. We are aware of great pain and suffering, injustice and abandonment, abuse and trauma. What we usually can't see and haven't understood up until now is that *these realities (that are part of the life we have created for ourselves) are not who we are. They are the outer reality we have created for ourselves unconsciously by the weaves that developed from our soulless and mindless thought forms, habits and emotional blueprints.* These are not part of our soul. They are born from thoughts we have had over thousands of lifetimes based on misunderstandings and misconceptions from the blinders we all wear.

The outer reality that these energy identities create acts to slowly bring every human down the path to conscious awareness, the path to understanding that instead, *what we are is the Pure Soul Essence of Originating Source.* The outer conditions then are not who we are, but are the conditions and situations that are present in order to open our eyes to our true reality. Even though the journey is complex and long, the path each of us takes eventually leads us to that knowledge. The pain and suffering we experience are only the expressions of our outer realities. They are the experiences we create to get ourselves to pay attention, the things that motivate us and ultimately bring us to consciousness. We do not need to spend lifetimes creating perfection, since we already are perfect. *We only have to realize that this is so.*

What Is the Next Step Then?

Now that we know at some intellectual level about the Pure Soul Essence, where do we go from here? Knowing about its presence does not do all that much. Many of you may not even be able to grasp this yet. And that is fine. This is a process, and we can't be at the end before we even begin.

I am confident that you've already been using the Pure Soul Essence as you have worked with the various exercises throughout *CHOICES*. Therefore, without knowing it, you have already begun the next step, where we start using the powerful energy to heal and recreate those outer conditions. These conditions create great blinders for us, and we often define others and ourselves through them. I truly hope all of you are doing the Key Exercise, as it's a powerful way to remove the blinders.

Now, though, I would like to encourage each of you to spend some time in the room that was hidden from you for so long. It is a wondrous place of balance, harmony, and serenity. It is peace. It is love. It is knowledge. It is faith. If you've had a bad day, you can move into that space on the drive home and bask in your own purity and calm. If you're having houseguests and the demands of being a hostess are overwhelming, *become one* with your Light. While baking or picking up your kids from school, ask that your Pure Soul Essence expand within, through and around you. Feel the energy and enjoy the Divine Order it brings. Expand your awareness by practicing the connection with Who You Truly Are on a daily basis in as many moments as you find. Do you need to change a diaper? Or print out a report for your boss? Or wait in line at the bank/post office/DMV? Grab these moments to become one with your Pure Soul Essence. It's not always necessary for you to feel that serenity and perfection. Merely speaking the words "I am one with my Pure Soul Essence" will put you in that energy field.

The Divine Energies

The Pure Soul Essence carries with it even more than you can probably imagine. It gives us access to all the Divine Energies that are within the Originating Source. We don't have to ask something or someone outside of ourselves to heal us, to give a loved one energy or to help us get a job. Since we are Soul Aspects of Originating Source, our Pure Soul Essence carries the entire range of energy and knowledge contained within our Creator.

As the Originating Source evolves, All There Is at that level is accessible to each and every one of us. We can ask for and utilize the energies any time we wish. Since they are generated from Originating Source, they are on a Spiritual Will frequency and cannot operate in any way but in the Highest Ideal for the situation or person they are meant to help. They cannot be manipulated to harm someone. However, keep in mind that because we are in the Free Will Kingdom, we must consciously access the Divine energies by asking. The Higher Selves or Originating Source may not give them to any human being without permission, since to do so would be a trespass of our free will. Yet when we call the Divine energies into our lives they are instantly brought in at the highest frequency level an individual can handle. Some of the important ones are Divine Love, Divine Forgiveness, Divine Word, Divine Mind, Divine Clarity and Divine Understanding. (For a longer list, please visit Appendix II.) How can we use them? Let me explain.

How to Use the Divine Energies

Think of a dam holding back billions of tons of water that just looks pretty when the dam's sluice gates are closed. When the gates are open and the water pours forth, there are huge benefits. The energy of the water moving through the dam generates millions of kilowatts of electricity, which helps power the communities around it. The water itself moves down a river that sustains wildlife and brings the water to outlying areas that need it for farming and the local population. Upon its release, the water becomes more than what it was when it was passive and dormant.

The same is true of our Pure Soul Essence. Within us is this potential power, but if we don't open up the sluice gates, it sits there available and untapped. What we do then is to open up the gates, which is actually very easy. To access our purest, most perfect power all we need is *focused thought*. Could it be that easy? Yes. When we focus our attention on the Pure Soul Essence, we become one with its energy (as described in Chapter Ten). Then, through thought, we can direct the energy to go where we need it. It can help us heal our lives on every level.

We control the energy by sending out the Light in its totality, or we can send out specific Divine streams of the energy. Picture a dam with many sluice gates. Sometimes one or a few are open, while other times all of them are open, depending on how much water is needed. With the Pure Soul Essence, you can send out the totality of All That Is and/or you can open one sluice gate with a specific Divine energy, sending that energy out alone. You can also activate two or more gates (with different Divine energies coming from each one) at the same time. Let me illustrate.

Exercise

Let's say you're having a major problem at work, and your boss is so busy that he/she doesn't spend the time to understand the problems affecting the completion of your assigned project. The boss only stops by for a minute to find out if you're finished and berates you for the delay without even allowing you to speak. Then he's off, only to repeat the scenario time and again. What are the issues here? There are elements of poor communication, frustration, and lack of understanding, to name a few. With each occurrence, you are getting more and more upset. What you can do (instead of or in addition to the other techniques you've already learned) is to activate the Divine Energies, either in the moment or later when you have mental space.

- First Amalgamate and then focus your thought on the Pure Soul Essence. You can use the symbol of water behind the dam if that helps. Then activate Divine Communication (to help heal the poor communication pattern), Divine Serenity (to help soothe the frustration), and Divine Understanding (to help bring understanding into the pattern where it is lacking on one or both sides) simply by thinking it. You say, "I activate Divine Communication, Divine Serenity, and Divine Understanding." This opens the gate and releases the Divine energies from your Pure Soul Essence. Simply direct the flow of energy out from your center into the outer condition on which you are working. You say, "I send the energy to the condition at work that is upsetting me." See, sense or imagine the energy move in, through and around the condition, bringing balance, harmony, and healing to it. Be sure to include your own physical and etheric bodies in the energy.

- Continue to focus on it for a minute or two. You don't need to push the energy out any more than someone needs to push the water out once the dam's sluice gate is opened. Activating the Divine energy creates an immediate powerful flow, whether you can 'see' it or not. The energy finds its target and does its work. It's never going to harm you or anyone else. It works in the Highest Ideal, as it will carry the exact frequency of energy needed for the situation. This work can be done in just a few minutes. Quick. Easy. Effortless.

If you don't know which energy to activate, out of all that are available for one situation or another, do your best and ask the Higher Selves to help you. If you ask them, they will call up the necessary Divine energy, even if you do not specify. I encourage you to explore and try it out, getting used to how it works. By activating one or several energies, when it feels appropriate, will help improve your outer conditions.

What's most important is that you use the energy! In conjunction with the Key Exercise, these energies will add speed and efficiency to the healing process in your life. You will find that the outer conditions (which have blinded you to who you truly are and have blocked you from having the life you want live) will begin to change, slowly at first and then with more momentum. You are in control. The more you tap into and use your Pure Soul Essence, the more you will benefit. Life is busy and complicated, so there will be times when it's easy to do this exercise and times when it's not. The Pure Soul Essence isn't going anywhere. It will always be there for you when you need it.

What Is the End Goal?

The end goal is to live in that Pure Soul Essence space on a moment-to-moment basis. To get there requires the neutralizing of all of our etheric bodies – the thought forms, the habits, and the emotional blueprints. When we are fully functioning out of that experience—from within the Pure Soul Essence—we are living the very highest, most perfect existence possible. We aren't there yet, but it will happen. Getting there is a wonderful trip, with incredible advantages, even if we haven't reached the end goal. I recommend that you not worry about the end and focus instead on where you're at any given time. Use the Pure Soul Essence energy to bring the possible into your life where you thought the impossible dwelled. I understand that sometimes a better life can feel unattainable. But you have the power, since you've discovered what's in the hidden room. You can simply open the door, flip the switch, and turn on the Light. Choose to make a better life for yourself.

Chapter Eighteen: Proper Self-Love

Higher Selves Quote

> *Practice the celebration of the self that unmarred, pure and perfect inner essence. Love your perfection. Love yourself. You don't have to have a reason to love yourself properly. You don't have to be the best man or the best woman on the block. You don't have to be in a state of absolute health. You don't have to be anything, because you already are perfection—separated from that perfection by the blueprints/habits/thoughts in the altered reality. They will not give you peace because you are not conscious of the fact that you are peace.*

One of the hardest things in life is to be happy with who we are. We are so often dissatisfied with how we look, the conditions in which we live and the inner world of our thoughts and feelings. In seeking happiness, we embark on a journey to fix, as best we can, what we don't like about ourselves. Because we feel that fixing ourselves is so difficult, real happiness seems illusive. We often feel like failures and sometimes even give up on life. So at first, Proper Self-Love may seem like an impossible dream, attainable for some but not for us. There seems to be too much wrong and no way to solve it. Is there help for us? Is there a solution to our dilemma?

The answer to how to love the self properly is to love the self properly.

Although that statement seems odd at first, you will soon see the truth in it. However, for you to understand it, I need to explain what Proper Self-Love means, why we misunderstand love, how we find Proper Self-Love and what it will do for us. This is the single most important chapter in *CHOICES*.

What Is Proper Self-Love?

Proper Self-Love is the conscious feeling, on a moment-to-moment basis, that you are the purity and perfection of your Pure Soul Essence. This total and anchored connection carries with it unconditional self-acceptance and love of who you truly are, as well as the conviction (beyond any doubt) that the situations and conditions in your life do not define you. It is the essence of peace, balance, harmony, joy and the miraculous. Proper Self-Love is enormously powerful and has the ability to heal and bring peace and harmony at every level of one's life.

If you properly love yourself, you do not have to *cultivate* the idea of faith within yourself. Faith is a constant companion. If you properly love yourself, you will not see yourself in a position of falling short or of doing or not doing what you or other people thought you should have done. With Proper Self-Love in place, every action is accepted as a reflection of your own perfection. It is the secret to joy and happiness.

Please don't confuse Proper Self-Love with egotism, narcissism or selfishness. Though they are part of the Human condition, they represent the distortions of love, not the ideal. By the end of the chapter, you will understand the difference.

The highest frequency level of Divine Love attainable within the Human Kingdom is called Higher Heart Consciousness. This means that Divine Love contains different frequencies of love. Divine Love reaches the souls in each Kingdom (Dimension) at the frequency level they can handle and process. Picture a prism that has Divine Love shining through it, with each level a different color. The lowest frequency would reach the Mineral Kingdom. The next level would reach the Plant Kingdom, etc. Higher Heart Consciousness is the level of love that all humanity can and must attain in order to continue its evolution toward higher Dimensions. Each Dimension above the Human Kingdom would be able to receive even higher frequency levels of Divine Love.

What then is Proper Self-Love? Proper Self-Love is part of Higher Heart Consciousness, as is Proper Love of Others, two sides of the same coin. Together, they are essential for every human to attain in order to graduate into the 5th Dimension. This is why love dominates our lives and plays such a major role in metaphysical and religious philosophies. Yet so many of our perspectives of love are skewed or limited in some manner, based on our misconceptions and false beliefs.

Love Misunderstood

In 99 cases out of 100, love manifests in our lives in ways that do not reflect the highest level of our potential to love. Our perceptions are colored, not only by every emotion and experience that we have processed in previous existences, but in this lifetime as well. So when we love, we love through the distortions of all those experiences.

It is difficult to clear up the misunderstandings of all that has gone into our concepts of loving (whether it be of yourself, another individual or groups of individuals) because the Emotional/Habit/Thought Form Bodies carry the complex and convoluted altered realities through which we perceive. Love must filter through the smog of these altered realities, losing its purity in the process. It is like playing telephone, where the clarity of the message (proper love) gets distorted and lost as it's processed through our misunderstandings, judgments and beliefs that reword and reshape the message (the feeling), to the point that the true meaning of love is lost by the time it makes its way through to our consciousness.

To clarify further, I will remind you of how the emotional blueprints work. You will recall that when an event happens, it triggers an already-established emotional response. We attach a response to the event or the experience and don't realize that the event is actually neutral. We are so used to combining the experience with the emotional response that we feel it is one and the same. This is true of all aspects of loving.

Therefore, what we find (using romantic love as an example) is that ideas and concepts about love are often skewed, impure and can be damaging. We all know of people who use love to control their lovers. There are also some that feel love is about self-sacrifice or who equate love with pain. Some feel that love is never to be trusted. Others feel that once discovered, love is a jewel that can never be found again and must be held captive, despite any negative indications. We make verbal attacks against our loved ones in the name of love, saying things like, "If you loved me, you wouldn't do..." or "How can you love me if you can treat me like..." There is also love that casts someone in the role as rescuer or someone else who feels duty bound to take responsibility for another. Then there is the age-old belief that once someone loves you, you will be happy. This list could go on for pages.

Whatever we carry at the thought form and emotional blueprint level determines how our own personal misunderstandings and distortions will play out, whether it is while loving others or loving ourselves. Yet, exactly how each one of us distorts love is not essential to know. You may have some idea of your own predispositions and false beliefs, and hopefully you will work on neutralizing those by doing the Key Exercise.

However, there are three elements related to loving the self properly that need to be addressed. They are simple but essential concepts to the understanding, use and attainment of Proper Self-Love. They are as follows:

You are NOT your Outer Conditions

I touched on this point in the Pure Soul Essence chapter, but it is essential that I hammer it home, since so many of us constantly judge ourselves negatively due to our outer conditions. What do I mean by outer conditions? And why is this concept so important to understand?

Our outer conditions are simply the things/people/experiences that are present in our lives. This chapter will address the negative conditions, but in fact, everything in your outer reality, good or bad, are parts of these outer conditions. Some of the millions of possible conditions we do not like having in our lives are money problems, relationship problems, health problems, communication problems, body image problems, etc. These conditions are the reason for our lack of self-acceptance and self-love. They fuel the constant self-criticisms that run rampant in our minds. They make us believe we are worthless or failures in some way. Because we confuse the conditions in our lives with being who we are, we hold ourselves prisoner to those conditions.

Therefore, to attain Proper Self-Love, we must clearly understand that *we are not our outer conditions*. Instead, we are pure and perfect expressions of the Totality of All That Is. *The Pure Soul Essence is who we truly are.* We are not our bank accounts, our broken love affairs or our overweight bodies. We are neither the chaos that surrounds us, nor anything else external that may be manifesting negatively in our lives.

Children are sometimes conditioned from very early on to feel unloved, rejected or unworthy, and this treatment takes a toll on a child's mind. But when these children become adults, they have the ability to understand that these harmful words and gestures have nothing at all to do with who they really are—the beautiful expressive Light of the Pure Soul Essence. Each individual can properly love one's self and live without judging what takes place in life, since the conditions are external and have no bearing on the pure expression of the soul. We can choose to not let the children within ourselves make decisions for the adults that we are.

This does not mean that you can live irresponsibly and carelessly. We are in the Free Will Kingdom, and each individual carries responsibility for one's self. When we understand the truth of this distinction, we have taken the first step toward loving the self properly.

In summary, although many of you had been aware that Proper Self-Love is an important goal, you may (as I did) have felt it would be an impossible task to love the negative patterns that had dogged you for so many years. If you think your flaws are so large, it seems impossible to ever love yourself. However, *Proper Self-Love is not about learning to love your flaws. It is about changing your perspective from defining yourself by your outer conditions to seeing yourself as the true purity and perfection you are.* Attainment of this new viewpoint is a much more reasonable goal and one that I am confident we can all accomplish. And when we do, we can truly move away from that loser, failure voice we have become so familiar with in life, the one fueled by the erroneous assumption that we are our outer conditions.

Proper Self-Love is Already Inside Us

Because you have read the previous chapter on the Pure Soul Essence, you now clearly understand the irony of it all. The very thing that you have felt was so elusive is the very thing for which you do not have to search, since we already carry it inside. There is no journey needed to get to Proper Self-Love. Just stay right where you are and it is yours.

Proper Self-Love is an energy we harness at that Pure Soul Essence level. You don't have to learn Self-Love from scratch or take years to search for it. There's no need to fix all your flaws to even begin to get there. Instead, you only need to know that this powerful love is already within you. It is available to you 24/7, whenever you may need it. And to connect to it is as simple as to become one with your Pure Soul Essence. Once in that space, just by focusing on Divine Love, Higher Heart Consciousness or on Proper Self-Love (the effect will be the same using any of them since they are all part of Divine Love) the energy begins to flow. You need only direct and use it in any manner you wish, just as you would any other Divine Energy.

When you start to use this Divine Love Energy you may not feel anything. The altered realities can be so densely shrouded that it is often difficult to feel the love in the beginning. But each time you access this love and work with it, you will move closer and closer to feeling it in your heart. However, even if we cannot feel it, its energy is as powerful and effective, as it would be if you had already fully accomplished Proper Self-Love (as defined above). We need only learn how to use the energy. It will bring the healing, balance and harmony into your life, remove your blinders and allow you to know who you truly are. In this way, we can attain Proper Self-Love by using the Divine Energy of Proper Self-Love.

We Can Heal Our Outer Conditions

Even though we won't properly love ourselves just by intellectually understanding what it means, since we have to truly connect with the idea, feeling that we *are* our Pure Soul Essence. Until then, however, we can use this Proper Self-Love energy to both help us remove the blinders that hide our perfection and to also recreate our outer realities.

What an idea! We can use Proper Self-Love even before we have truly attained it! It is not only possible but also important and will lead us to where we all want to go. Proper Self-Love brings tremendous healing into our body and into life's difficult conditions and circumstances. If you cultivate an intimate love affair with your inherent Higher Heart Consciousness, it will open all doors for higher levels of emotional stability and will create truly loving conditions in your life pattern. Proper Self-Love radiates out into the totality of all that you are, all that you have, and all that you touch. It is that Divine Energy that lifts everything and everyone into higher and higher levels. Regardless of where you believe you are, the Proper Self-Love energy will allow you to recreate the fabric of all your external conditions that, up to now you believed were inescapable.

Proper Self-Love and Loving Others

Before I lead you through the process that will help you access and use your own Divine Proper Self-Love, I would briefly like to mention how the energy will also affect your relationships with others. To love another person properly, you must first truly properly love yourself. (You can't save a man from drowning if you don't first learn how to swim.) However, as you activate and bathe in your own Higher Heart Consciousness on a consistent basis, you will slowly move toward properly loving the self. And as you do this, you will be able to attract others whose proper self-love is equivalent to yours.

In time, Proper Acceptance and Love of your own Pure Soul Essence will enable you to recognize and honor the Pure Soul Essence of others (whether it be a personal intimate relationship, someone with whom you work or a transitory relationship with someone you pass on the street). Once you know and feel that you are pure and perfect, it will become impossible not to see that every other individual is also pure and perfect. Judgments, prejudice, bias and hate are no longer possible to feel. Just as you Properly Love yourself and you know that you are not your outer conditions (manifestations), you will Properly Love others in their purity, knowing that they are not the sum of their outer conditions either. As you stand in the center of the purity and acceptance of all life, peace becomes possible because you feel peaceful. Healing becomes possible because you have healed yourself from within.

This may all seem too idealistic and far-fetched a goal for humanity. However, this is the goal for us to reach in order to give us all that we truly desire. Getting there may not happen overnight, but each step we take towards that end brings immediate rewards. We do not have to be at the end to get great benefits. How do we take those steps? Let's take a look.

Processing Proper Self-Love

We begin where we are with one step, then another step and another. Before reading the following Conscious Meditation, please choose a circumstance in your life that makes you dissatisfied. You will use this circumstance as you participate in the exercise. I will lead you through the exercise to help you experience at the feeling level, that *you are not your outer conditions/the specific circumstance you have chosen.* Then, you will activate the flow of your Proper Self-Love. (We will open the dam of Pure Soul Essence by activating the Divine Love gate.) And, you will direct this Love to heal your outer circumstances. These are easy steps, and by the end of the meditation, you will experience them. From then on, you will be able to fully utilize this powerful energy on your own, enhancing the healing process within your life.

Please note that sending Divine Love into a difficult situation does not mean that you are adding power to a negative condition. Instead, the Love brings those negative conditions into a state of balance. As was suggested in Chapter Ten, you can either read the Conscious Meditation or have someone read it to you. Whichever way you choose, focus on the words and the energy is yours to use.

CONSCIOUS MEDITATION

Proper Self-Love

Please stand in the center of your Pure Soul Essence. Picture the Light within, the Light that is symbolic of the essence of each and every one of you, your Aspect of the Totality of Originating Source. You can imagine it, think it or say it, as you expand the

Light to encompass the whole of your physical body and etheric bodies. Become one with the Light, as it brings to every part of you the balance, harmony and perfection that you are. In this state of oneness with your Pure Soul Essence, project into the Originating Source of All That Is and amalgamate with the Totality of your Higher Selves. Feel the energy flowing through your being. Become aware of the beacon of Light you have become in this amalgamated state and that you are sharing this Light with anyone around you. Take a few moments and feel this state of purity and perfection. If you cannot yet feel it, imagine how it might feel. Focus on this place of balance and serenity.

♥♥♥

Once you are connected with the true you, please focus on the Higher Heart Consciousness Energy carried within your Pure Soul Essence. This focus activates the flow of Divine Love at the highest frequency attainable in the Human Kingdom. Ask that it move in, through and around the totality of your being—into the physical body and into all your etheric bodies. Feel it or sense it in any way that you do. You can think of Divine Love as if you are snuggling up in pink, loving clouds that nourish and nurture you. Another way to imagine it is to see yourself as bathing in pink light. Say to yourself, "I Love Myself Properly. I Love Others Properly. Others Love Me Properly." Please spend a few moments with those thoughts in your mind. These thoughts, created while you are amalgamated with your Pure Soul Essence, do more than just empower the Proper Self-Love thought form. Because of the Amalgamation, the focus of attention activates the flow of the powerful Divine Love energy. This energy is more powerful than a single thought. *It is the most powerful healing energy in the Human Kingdom.* Feel the Love in every fiber and molecule of your being.

♥♥♥

The next step is to focus on the specific situation in your life that greatly dismays you. Are you unhappy with your body? Your state of health? Your job? Your mate? Your financial condition? Visualize the condition located outside and in front of you. Picture it in your mind's eye. It may be black and shapeless or some other representation that works for you. But it is clearly outside you and not attached to you. Once you have that inner visual set, leave your Pure Soul essence and mentally project into the misery of the condition. Consciously say, "I project into the outer condition in my life of…(whatever you have chosen)." You will not empower its negativity while you do this since the Higher Selves protect you while amalgamated. Focus on what you are feeling/sensing/seeing inside this condition. Feel the pain or the shame or the fear that the condition brings up for you. Stand in the center of those feelings. Become conscious of how unloving you really are toward yourself. Listen to the thoughts that come up. Are you questioning if you can ever love this part of yourself? Are you feeling like a failure? Are you blaming yourself or others for your problem? Are you convinced that you are a loser, a whiner, or a basket case? No matter what comes up for you, please notice the discomfort, the despair, the powerlessness or the hopelessness you feel as you are connecting with this part of your outer reality. You are not to do anything else with it at this point except experience the problem in the moment.

♥♥♥

Now please return to your Pure Soul Essence and the healing bath of Proper Self-Love. To think it is to create it, so think the thought, "I project back into the center of my Pure Soul Essence." Feel the difference. Feel a return to peace and serenity. Feel the perfection that you are. This purity is yours and is separate from your outer reality. It is there for you to access at any time. Focus again on the words of Proper Self-Love. Say, "I love myself properly." Consciously continue to activate the flow of Divine Love within yourself. Feel yourself back in the pink cloud of love. Remain conscious of the distinction between the true you and the painful outer condition that has been created by your altered realities. If you have difficulty experiencing this distinction, visualize a symbolic moat or space between your purity and the problematic outer condition so it doesn't crowd in on you. This symbol can sometimes help us feel the difference more clearly. Use it or any other symbol that may help you. And continue to feel the Love.

Now that you have experienced the difference between the true you as opposed to your outer conditions, we are going to use Divine Love to heal the outer condition you have been working with. While centered within the Pure Soul Essence, direct the Love out to this condition. Say, "I send the Proper Self-Love out to engulf and surround and heal the condition of…" See, sense or imagine the Love surrounding this condition, including all those unloving thoughts about yourself, judgments, criticisms, and negative emotions related to it. Flood your Higher Heart Consciousness into the false beliefs, misunderstandings and misconceptions that were part of the condition. Allow the Divine Love energy to heal the distortions—the feelings of imperfection—and to bring those into a state of balance. The self-judgments, hurts, despair and lack of self-acceptance are now being held within the Divinely Loving energy. Your outer conditions have no affect on you. They are not who you truly are. They are the creations of your altered realities and are now being healed with your Love.

♥♥♥

Finally, consciously give yourself permission to Love yourself. Bask in the feeling, meaning, and energy of Love at its highest level—Love that makes no demands, love that is supportive, Love that is healing, Love that is balanced, Love that accepts all. Consciously focus on the highest level of Love and lay claim to it for yourself. Lay claim to the greater vision Love carries with it. Lay claim to the joy that Love is. Lay claim to having Love in your life on a moment-to-moment basis. Practice and cultivate consciously Loving yourself.

End of Meditation

Proceeding from Here

I recommend that you continue to work in a state of consciousness with Proper Self-Love. Simply sit and practice standing in the center of this Pure Soul Essence Divine Energy. There is no need to repeat the part where you jump back and forth between the outer condition and the Pure Soul Essence. That was in the meditation to help you understand and feel the distinction. What's important now is to reconnect on a regular basis to the Love that you carry within. When a situation comes to mind that causes you emotional discomfort, you can return immediately to the center of your Pure Soul Essence, activate and send Love to your being, the situation and/or the other person. Even if you don't remember to do it in the moment, doing it whenever you think of it is powerful and healing. If you work conscientiously while amalgamated to send Divine Love to your outer reality, (including the people and the beliefs that are part of the condition/s), you will experience the power of Love as it transforms your life.

Proper Self-Love is already within us. You don't need to force yourself to love the upsetting situations in your life in order to find this love and use it. Instead, you can connect to the love within yourself from this moment forward. You can clear your mind of the finish-line mentality, thinking that you have failed or will fail because you haven't gotten there or will never get there. Higher Heart Consciousness is powerful on every level and with every step taken. Every step moves our life forward. Each time we stand in the center of the Proper Self-Love energy and send it outward, that powerful frequency moves into every symbolic crack in our layers of altered realities and works to heal our lives.

Why Is Such an Important Chapter Last?

This is easy to answer. The reason is twofold. First, this chapter contains concepts that had to be explained in the earlier chapters. Each chapter builds on the ones before it, and this chapter was the end result. Secondly, having read the earlier chapters, you can see that you can apply the Higher Heart Consciousness energy to many of the things you've already learned about. By just reviewing the chapter titles in the book, you will find many areas/opportunities to use love for healing. You can work on loving the chaos in your life or the beliefs and judgments that hold you prisoner. How about flowing the love into the Thought Form, Habit, and Emotional Bodies? Or you could address any areas of emotionalizing and targeting that are giving you a hard time. Then there is the one we can all use the loving energy on—the material imbalance that is almost always present in our lives.

Do not forget to work with the Key Exercise as well. This exercise is essential too. If we do the neutralizing, we will work through the layers of our misunderstandings (the blinders that keep us from fully achieving Proper Self-Love) and will create even more openings for the Divine Love to penetrate. By working with the Key Exercise and the Proper Self-Love energy simultaneously, we will more quickly create the results we want in life. It is exciting. It is powerful. And it is worth it!

Final Words

Higher Selves Quote

The thing to remember is that we chose—whether in ignorance or with the unconscious knowledge that we could grow from those experiences—the patterns we manifest in this lifetime. In this respect, we must take full responsibility for where we are right now, consciously putting aside all self-blame, consciously putting aside judgment of ourselves or others, and understand that in this moment, we can take full responsibility for our lives.

By taking responsibility, we have taken the first step toward true *choice*. Once we look to ourselves to solve our problems, we find the real source of our power. We don't blame. Instead, our problems bring awareness and motivation to move forward.

Higher Selves Quote

Remember, we think that we control our lives because we are awake and our eyes are open. But in reality we are reactive. We are only hosts for these altered realities that live in our Thought Form Bodies – they are the bosses and we are the hosts.

Self-awareness and motivation to move forward has brought us to the point of learning about how our life—our outer reality—is created by us. Our problems have been the unwitting result of our ignorance about how our etheric bodies weave our outer conditions.

Higher Selves Quote

For once the thought has been projected and becomes a part of the Thought Form Body, and once that thought form has been fed and fueled by other thoughts that are like itself, it then moves out to create, within this altered reality, a life that will match itself. When it gains enough strength, it brings forth its form outward, into our physical world.

Our thoughts, from this life and all prior lifetimes, have reinforced and created complex altered realities that we carry with us at all times. Soulless and mindless, they operate to empower themselves, to gain enough energy to manifest into the physical reality.

Higher Selves Quote

The process of being aware is one of attempting to live your life with its familiar patterns and finding them no longer satisfactory. These patterns are so deeply ingrained that most of the time there has been no conscious thought put into them. We simply play them out over and over because of their familiarity. And yet it is in this reality where consciousness of who you really are must be born.

At some point, we decide that we are no longer willing to accept the patterns that manifest repeatedly in our lives. And we begin the search for answers. This journey led to *CHOICES*—led me to write it and you to read it. We understand the significance of the Key Exercise. We know that just thinking positively is not enough to manifest profound and lasting change. We know we need to neutralize the negative energy identities that have dogged us for lifetimes and also to empower the positive thought forms. We now actively make conscious choices to help ourselves.

Higher Selves Quote

> *It's interesting that in this reality we may feel we do not have faith, but most often we have faith in the oddest things. You take your automobile to the mechanic and you leave it there in good faith that it will be fixed. You do not go running back to check to see what's going on. You sit in the chair, having faith that the chair will hold you up. So you do have faith, but not in yourself.*

There is often emphasis on the external ways to seek help, seek assistance, have faith in, have belief in, so that many individuals think they are helpless when it comes to affecting changes or loving themselves. Yet this belief literally imprisons individuals and holds them in place, creating conditions that do not allow them to live a happy, joyful, loving existence. We focus outward toward an authority figure and yet it is within ourselves that lives the authority. Within ourselves lives the purest, highest, most perfect expression—our Pure Soul Essence. Begin to love yourself.

It is clear. We need to acknowledge our perfection within. We need to also work with our Pure Soul Essence and Proper Self-Love to take off our blinders. The awareness, understanding and proper use of the Divine within us is the goal of all humanity. It is richly rewarding and monumentally powerful.

Higher Selves Quote

We caution you not to be disillusioned when all circumstances do not fly smoothly. This is not an indication of wrongdoing or error on the part of anyone, but a working through of the patterns in order to achieve neutrality—neutrality being the state of absolute centeredness. There is no way to achieve that centeredness without also processing those patterns that separate us from the sense of centeredness.

We will still have problems in our lives. This is part of the process. These problems are opportunities to discover what false beliefs and unconscious altered realties we still harbor. We cannot clear all the thoughts, habits and blueprints from thousands of lifetimes overnight. Yet with each step we take, we are helping ourselves. Again, in one year, we will be one year older. Let us be one year older and improved in many areas of our lives instead of remaining in the stagnation and misery of the status quo.

Higher Selves Quote

We also ask this group to consider that these Wednesday-night sessions are not long enough to reveal the totality of all Information. We present information; we do not present a dogmatic limited reality. We give you seeds, and we ask that you take these seeds and use the "I have" of the mind to make these seeds grow.

I ask the same of all my readers. I have given you some powerful seeds to think about and utilize. Please work with your Higher Selves and your Pure Soul Essence to find answers and solutions to any questions or difficulties you may encounter. Know that if you have the question, you also have the answer.

Conclusion

To conclude, I will make one more suggestion: I recommend that you think seriously about getting a group together, where you can meet on a regular basis to practice and share what you are experiencing. The group may be you and only one other person who is also interested or perhaps there could be several people. The numbers don't matter. If you're already in a group of some sort, you may want to introduce this information.

Not only is having a good support system a way to remind us to keep working and have hope, but helping each other is also positive. Doing the exercises together does not need to be a somber task. It can be fun as you go through the ups and down. It can also mean interesting insights and the discovery of gifts and talents for each of you.

It is essential not to judge one another. Everyone has his or her own unique patterns. Some participants may be vulnerable and willing to talk about their problems. Others will keep theirs close to the vest and will rarely, if ever, share. Some will only show up one or two times, and that will be it, while others will attend every time. Often someone else will see our patterns more quickly and easily than we can. It is the support and understanding from those present that can make your process seem less scary or foreign.

Everyone in the group, whether ready or not to move forward on an issue, will have the benefit of having seeds of healing planted, which will blossom over time as the soul is ready. The group will also engender new ideas and insights. New exercises will be developed. In fact, everyone will benefit. Group hugs, a touch, tears and smiles are a healing bonus. Neither a requirement nor something to do instead of our own individual work, group work can add energy and effectiveness to the process.

I wish you all a wonderful journey to better lives!

Glossary: Metaphysical Terms Used in *CHOICES*

1st Dimension – The first level of evolutionary soul consciousness/awareness. It consists of the Mineral Kingdom (the planets) and is governed by instinctive will.

2nd Dimension – The second level of evolutionary soul consciousness/awareness. It consists of the Plant Kingdom (the flora) and is governed by instinctive will.

3rd Dimension – The third level of evolutionary soul consciousness/awareness. It consists of the Animal Kingdom (the fauna) and is governed by instinctive will.

4th Dimension – The fourth level of evolutionary soul consciousness/awareness. It consists of the Human Kingdom (incarnate and disincarnate) and is governed by free will.

5th Dimension – The fifth level of evolutionary soul consciousness/awareness. It consists of the Inner-Planetary Kingdom (Inner-Planetaries/5th Dimensionals) and is governed by spiritual will. All humans eventually 'graduate' into this Dimension.

5th Dimensionals – The overall term that refers to the souls that inhabit the 5th Dimension.

6th Dimension – The sixth level of evolutionary soul consciousness/awareness. It consists of the Spiritual Hierarchy Kingdom and is governed by spiritual will.

7th Dimension – The seventh level of evolutionary soul consciousness/awareness. It is governed by spiritual will. There is yet to be much information about this Dimension.

Altered Reality – A very real environment, created and inhabited by thought forms.

Amalgamation – The joining or blending of your own energy field with the energy field of the Higher Selves and/or the Originating Source. This term is also used by the Higher Selves to describe when an individual becomes one with their Pure Soul Essence.

Animal Kingdom – (*See definition for 3rd Dimension.*)

Aspects – Parts of a soul that have 'broken off' to live their own individual existences. Each part is separate but equal in that each Aspect contains the Totality of the Originating Source.

Aspecting – The action of a soul dividing into separate but equal individual parts.

Conscious Meditation – The process of remaining conscious and in the now while receiving information from the Higher Selves so that the information can be brought into your everyday world on a moment-to-moment basis. (In classic meditation practices information is taken in at the subconscious level, while in the alpha state. In most cases, it remains buried there so that you don't have **access to it on a moment-to-moment basis.)**

Conscious or Consciousness – 1.) An attempt to focus on specific thoughts or a specific state of mind without the distraction of transient thoughts. 2.) The level of soul awareness.

Creative Body – An envelope of energy surrounding each human being that contains all of the soul's potential creations as they exist at this point in time. The Creative Body uses the thought forms and habit imprints (see definitions) to slowly weave the pattern that will ultimately manifest into your physical reality. It is here that your outward physical life *is manufactured.* This manufacturing process takes place over a period of time prior to its manifestation into the physical realm. It is this Creative Body that can be read to determine what you are creating for your future.

Creative Life Force Energy –The compelling force within All That Exists. It is an impersonal energy that creates based on the nature and quality of the *fuel* it has to work with. Its *fuel* in the Human Kingdom consists of thought forms, habit imprints, and the emotional blueprints we carry.

De-Intensifying – The process of lowering an energy frequency level.

Divine Frequencies – Energy (in its purest form) that comes directly from Originating Source and pertains to a specific aspect of evolution in its Totality (e.g., Divine Love, Divine Forgiveness, and Divine Mind).

Dimensions – Frequency levels that represent the Evolutionary stages of a soul.

Emotional Blueprints – Patterns held in the Emotional Body that govern how we will respond emotionally to any given situation. A blueprint is a response pattern built up from previous lifetimes. The conglomerates of all the similar emotional responses have become the emotional blueprints. In this lifetime when an event occurs, a response pattern is triggered, releasing an emotional reaction from the past that greatly colors (discolors) how we experience the event in the present.

Note: When you do work within the Emotional Body, you are neutralizing the blueprint, not the emotions themselves.

Emotional Body – An envelope of energy (energy field) surrounding each human being in which our emotional blueprints are held.

Emotionalizing – Unconsciously being consumed by an emotion and therefore not consciously controlling the experience in the moment. (By being aware of emotionalizing, one can try to stand impartially and see the emotion for what it is.)

Energy Identities – Another term for thought forms. (*See definition for Thought Forms.*)

Etheric – A general term that refers to the non-physical plane and is often used by the Higher Selves when referring to the space containing the Thought Form Body, Habit Body, Emotional Body and Creative Body.

Etheric Bodies – The Thought Form Body, Emotional Body, Habit Body and Creative Body that occupy the etheric space around the physical body.

Free Will – The energy level of the 4th Dimension that gives every individual total and complete power and responsibility for all circumstances surrounding their lives. No trespassing of any human soul's free will can occur, since what happens to a soul must have conscious or unconscious agreement.

Habit Body – An envelope of energy (energy field) surrounding each human being in which our habit imprints reside.

Habit Imprints – Imprints that are created in the Habit Body based on the consistency of our thoughts as they occur lifetime after lifetime. Habit imprints carry no conscious thought, though they can be deeply ingrained. This is why a soul will experience the same conditions that have been played out over lifetimes. With each expression of the condition, the habit imprint is reinforced. The thought form impresses the Habit Body, which in turn reinforces the thought form itself, and the cycle continues.

Higher Heart Consciousness –This is the highest level of Divine Love attainable within the 4th Dimensional Human Kingdom. It is the level that all humans must reach prior to graduating to the 5th Dimension.

Higher Selves – 5th Dimensionals who consciously project thought, in a de-intensified frequency, into the Human Kingdom in order to assist in the evolutionary process of the four lower kingdoms. It is important to note that the Higher Selves cannot trespass the free will.

Human Kingdom – (*See definition for 4th Dimension.*)

Human Kingdom Heavens – The etheric space that houses disincarnate human souls who are in between lifetimes in the physical body.

In Frequency – The process a human uses in order to enter into and communicate with the Higher Selves at the 5th Dimensional level.

Instinctive Will – The energy level of the 1st, 2nd and 3rd Dimension relating to how the souls on these levels go through their evolutionary process based on impulses, genetic programming and instinctual behavior. It is Divine Will at the unconscious level.

Law of Magnetic Attraction – Describes the magnetic quality of thought forms that create our outer reality.

Light – The symbol that is most often used to represent and activate the very real energy of the Pure Soul Essence.

Manifesting – Creating in your outer reality that which is contained in your etheric bodies.

Mineral Kingdom – (*See definition for 1st Dimension.*)

Neutrality – 1.) The state of mind between belief and disbelief and between truth and untruth. 2.) The perfect balance of opposite polarities of thoughts (e.g., love and un-love).

Originating Source –This is another term for God/Allah/ Universal Source, etc. It is used instead of the more common words, since it is free of personal connotations and personal bias.

Pattern Healing – Healing that refers to the neutralizing and balancing of recurring sets of conscious and unconscious actions and reactions repeated through one's lifetime.

Plant Kingdom – (*See definition for 2nd Dimension.*)

Proper Self-Love – The cultivation of a strong, positive and conscious relationship to the self, based on our true perfect identity and not on our outward expression. It is the internal, complete awareness and acceptance of the perfection and beauty of one's Pure Soul Essence. Therefore, it contains no self-judgment. Proper Self-Love is half of Higher Heart Consciousness, with the other half being Proper Love of Others.

Pure Soul Essence – The Divine part of every soul that is a part of and directly connected to Originating Source. It is the highest, purest, most perfect part of each soul. Moving into your Pure Soul Essence activates the connection to the Originating Source and allows access to all knowledge, wisdom, and power from the highest Totality of All That Exists.

Soul – A soul is the minds of its past. It carries the energy of conscious awareness. As the soul evolves, it moves into higher and higher states of consciousness.

Spiritual Will – The energy level of the 5th, 6th, and 7th Dimensions relating to the fact that souls on these levels operate according to Divine Will, having made the conscious (as opposed to the instinctual) choice to do so.

Symbolism – The use of words, shapes or pictures to unleash into your own vibration the energy that is represented by the symbol. The use of symbolism, while powerful and necessary, often creates a 'phenomenon' that erroneously locks into the symbol itself rather than the very real energy the symbol represents. Symbolism is the powerful tool that we as humans have to access and manipulate energy that exists at an etheric level.

Thought Form Body – An envelope of energy (energy field) surrounding each human being, in which every thought from every lifetime resides.

Thought Forms – Energy identities that are created at the etheric level from every thought a soul has ever had. Soulless and mindless, each energy identity magnetically attracts similar thoughts, resulting in the existence of millions of these identities. They live within the Thought Form Body, and while they are invisible, they are nevertheless very real (for thought is energy in the same manner as your body is energy). Once created, a thought form immediately moves out, builds energy, and empowers itself by taking in every thought that is similar to it, whether it comes from the soul that created it or from others who direct similar thoughts toward you.

Unconscious – The envelopes of etheric energy known as the Thought Form Body, Habit Body, Emotional Body and Creative

Body that surround the physical body of every person throughout their evolutionary sojourn. If one is not consciously focused on their thoughts, the unconscious is allowed free rein.

Appendix I: Joan Culpepper

Quote: Anonymous

An optimist is a person who sees only the lights in the picture, whereas a pessimist sees only the shadows. An idealist, however, is one who sees the light and the shadows, and in addition sees something else: the possibility of changing the picture, of making the lights prevail over the shadows.

Joan Culpepper's life was dedicated to bringing light into the shadows. She was a pioneer. She went beyond the normal to the other side of possibility. And she did so by using her determination and talent to draw in the high levels of information from the 5th Dimension.

Childhood

Joan Culpepper was born one of three children in the Deep South of Tennessee. Feeling like she never fit in, she considered herself the black sheep of her family, and it's this sense of isolation and separation that may have been what led her to search for meaning in her life.

Joan was brought up as an Orthodox Southern Baptist, and early on she became disillusioned with the teachings of her church. "I had 'outgrown' the church at about age six, when I began to question the 'hellfire and damnation' aspects of the God I was taught," she said. "I was never able to put together the gentle soul of the man, Jesus, with a God who seemed unrelenting in his desire to punish. I learned early to repress my questions after being told, 'You will understand when you grow older.'" Unable to set aside her confusion, she began to search for answers. At first, she was drawn to the aspects of Christianity that concentrated on goodness and hope. Though she had no exposure as a child to ideas outside of a traditional religious setting, she was eventually drawn to different philosophies and viewpoints due to her great curiosity.

The Move to Los Angeles

In 1966, at the age of 31, Joan moved to the Los Angeles area. It was there that she first had a sense of 'coming home' and found people with whom she could truly communicate. She also finally began to understand the psychic experiences with which she had been blessed for most of her life, but had never been able to share.

Joan considered herself a "conscious spiritual seeker" and went from teacher to teacher, thought to thought, philosophy to philosophy, searching for the answers to her many questions about existence. She never stopped pursuing alternative ways of looking at the universe and our place in it, and described herself in this discovery process as "a true metaphysical groupie."

She went to group meditation meetings, became interested in self-hypnosis, and even experienced (as many of us have in our own search) the downside of some of these types of groups. In 1975 she became involved with the Heaven's Gate cult of Bo and Peep. It was soon clear, however, that her search for ultimate truth could not thrive in this cult structure "I was subsequently flunked by the two leaders when it was discovered that I was less a follower and more of a hindrance," Joan said. "After being excused permanently from this cult, I set up a halfway house for their ex-followers." She later joined with a group of ex-members of Jim Jones' Peoples Temple to form the Human Freedom Center, a non-profit organization dedicated to helping ex-cult members reenter mainstream society.

Joan never attempted to whitewash her brief involvement in Heaven's Gate nor did she try to lessen the roles that Bo and Peep played in the disruption of so many lives. When asked by reporters what would cause a group of people to buy into a UFO cult she always replied, "You would have to understand the psychology of the spiritual seeker in order to have that question answered properly."

Her positive and negative spiritual experiences throughout life gave her tremendous insights into herself and led her to come to the following conclusion: "The moral, if there is one, would seem to be that a good 'conscious spiritual seeker' never lets a good lesson or a bad experience go to waste. He does his best to find out how and why he ever got into it in the first place, what he can learn from it, and how he can prevent it from happening to him again."

It was clear that her hard-earned philosophies came at a price. From her own point of view she "developed a skepticism over the years, which most people viewed as cynical." Still, it strongly motivated her to take responsibility for getting her own information. She knew she had to step up to the plate.

Joan's Metaphysical Career Begins

Extremely intelligent, having graduated from her high school fourth in her class, Joan made her living during her twenties and thirties as an executive administrator, first at a TV station, then in advertising for a radio station. Soon she found herself drawn to the Tarot cards. She bought a book and a deck and learned the meanings of each card. She used her friends as guinea pigs and volunteered to do readings at parties. From time to time she would put the cards away for a few months when life was difficult. And each time she took them out again, her psychic ability would be at a higher level. In fact, the first time she took the cards down from the closet shelf after putting them away, she found she didn't need the book anymore. The second time it happened she knew ahead of time what the spread would be. Eventually, she advanced to the level where she could put out all the cards at once for every reading. At this point the cards were simply focal points that moved her into the psychic energy field.

In a relatively short time, Joan developed a reputation for her ability and had a large clientele, including Academy Award winners, best-selling authors, songwriters, businessmen, lawyers, doctors and psychiatrists. She also conducted meditation groups, seminars, and was a speaker/lecturer.

Discovering the Higher Selves

During Joan's journey into Tarot card readings, she was never quite satisfied and consistently asked the Originating Source for the highest level of information possible. By the mid-'70s, her ability to 'hear' improved to the point where she could hear her Higher Selves. She was as surprised as everyone around her, and at first didn't fully understand what she was receiving. There was even a reluctance based in uncertainty and fear of the unknown. Yet Joan didn't give up. She persevered and developed a very strong relationship with her Higher Selves.

It's hard to describe exactly how Joan did it. The process of her getting information was not like the channeling often done by mediums, nor did it involve psychic visions of any sort. Instead, Joan shifted her consciousness into the 5th Dimensional energy field, and from there she received the information as clearly as hearing it in person. Joan called it "being in frequency." When sharing the information, she spoke without any 'ums' or 'ers,' as if she was reading from a teleprompter. At times she would pause and ask the Higher Selves for clarity on an issue, and then after listening for a few seconds, she would continue. Sometimes when in frequency, Joan would relate the information in the first person, as if she were speaking as the Higher Selves. At other times, she would relate the information using the term "we" so as to include herself as part of the group she was speaking to. The quotes in the book show it done both ways.

Once Joan's connection with the 5th Dimensional level was clear and consistent, the psychic readings for her clients changed. Though she continued to use the Tarot cards for what she called the mundane portion of the readings, she began to incorporate Higher Self information that pertained directly to the individual. She called this part of the reading the soul scan.

How Joan's Work Expanded

Soon thereafter, Joan had the Higher Selves lead her Wednesday-night group, which they called the Conscious Meditation group. The Higher Selves worked with the class week after week to help us receive our own information consciously in the moment. They explained that with the increasing chaos, due to the speed up of evolutionary time, we needed to get answers and solutions in consciousness. They also showed us the need and the way to take responsibility for our own lives and helped us understand the deeper meaning of destiny and of life.

Over the months and years that followed, Joan added more classes and activities. She led a contact class that focused even more on helping us get our own information, both from the

Higher Selves and psychically. It would be nice if we could just pick up the phone and give a call to the 5th Dimension, but it doesn't work that way, and most of us needed help. Then, because she had gotten so much information from the soul scans of hundreds of individual readings, she pulled it all together and gave us a class on the Universe, which explained how souls evolved.

But Joan didn't stop there. The Higher Selves got her involved with 5th Dimensional healing work and also moved her into an arena of working with entity attachments. Attachments occasionally happen when someone who has died (an entity) becomes 'attached' to people living here in body. (This is not the same as possession!) Joan's group helped these entities make the decision to detach (as they had to freely agree to it), to gain evolutionary understanding and to guide them on how to help other souls on the other side. In fact, Joan, with the Higher Selves leading the way, was instrumental in helping many thousands of disincarnate (out-of-body) souls continue to evolve, shades of Ghost Whisperer, though involving real people.

Joan's View of Herself

Joan never courted publicity, although there were many opportunities. She believed that people who were meant to work with her would eventually find her. She also came to a firm understanding that all religions/philosophies taught many great truths, though the interpretations could vary from one to another. She saw that there are many roads souls could take to find the answers, and that she was just one of those roads. Joan understood and valued that there are many ways to find the hope, solace, help, understanding, and growth needed for the human condition, with each person finding his/her own pathway.

Overall, Joan liked to think of herself not just as a practicing psychic but also as a "meta-philosopher," who spoke Earth language with a cosmic accent. This simply meant that while her psychic energies were rooted in some higher cosmic arrangement, she used them in practical, pragmatic and down-to-earth ways. She sometimes was referred to as a "soul psychologist" by some of her clients since she used her abilities to bring understanding and insight into a client's life challenges based on the soul scans from the Higher Selves. She was a significant catalyst in bringing many to consciousness, waking them up to their own personal power. It is this practical side and self-help orientation of her information that is the basis for *CHOICES*.

In the mid-'90s Joan retired from her spiritual work and became a full-time grandmother to her daughter's twin girls. In 2006, she died very young, well loved and well remembered. Those of us who use her information, have improved our lives on so many levels. Joan is now working on the other side to help us in other ways. Her family has allowed this grateful author complete access to the entire body of her Higher Self work, spanning almost 20 years. It was Joan's desire that this information be shared with a wider audience. Her legacy belongs to us all. In Joan's own words, her deep understanding led her to see that "*...there is only one teacher and one truth, and it lies within the soul of every seeker, not without.*"

We can take what she gave us, use it, share it and create with it. *CHOICES* is written in her honor.

Appendix II: Generic Life Patterns

The following patterns are so common that we call them generic. Even if it seems like we don't experience a pattern, we find ourselves working on it anyway, as it is more than possible we have had it in a past life.

Addictions
Aging, death and dying
Anger / Irritation / Grudges / Rage
Abuse
Bigotry
Blame of self or others
Boundary issues
Co-dependence / Enmeshment
Control: too much, not enough
Criticism of self or others
Defensiveness
Depression
Disappointment / Discouragement
Disconnection from Self
Don't Fit In / Invisible
Entitlement
Failure
Fatigue, Tiredness
Fears and Anxiety
Financial Instability, Lack, Debt
Guilt
Half-empty Syndrome
Hatred
Health Issues / Illness
Helplessness
Hopelessness
Inactivity / Inertia
Inability to…
Inequity Patterns
Inferiority
Intolerance / Discrimination
Isolation
Judgment of self or others
Lack of Consciousness
Lack of Focus
Lack of Self-awareness
Lack of Self-connection

Lack of Self-discipline
Lack of Self-esteem
Lack of Self-responsibility
Lack of Self-worth
Lying
Mental Illness
Misconception / Misunderstanding
Misuse of Power
Over-rationalize, Over-justify
Powerlessness
Rejection (fear of)
Relationship issues
Resistance to....
Sadness / Hurts / Pain
Self-abuse
Self-blame
Self-doubt
Self-hatred
Self-judgment
Self-sabotage
Self-sacrifice
Shame
Targeting
Underachievement
Unrealistic expectations
Unwillingness to…
Victim and/or Victimization
Wilfulness
Worthlessness

Appendix III: Divine Energies

Divine Abundance, Divine Wealth, Financial Security
Divine Balance
Divine Clarity
Divine Communication
Divine Creativity
Divine Enlightenment
Divine Faith & Hope
Divine Focus
Divine Forgiveness
Divine Fulfillment
Divine Harmony
Divine Healing & Health
Divine Intention
Divine Joy
Divine Justice
Divine Love
Divine Material Balance
Divine Mind
Divine Neutrality
Divine Objectivity
Divine Order
Divine Purity of Purpose
Divine Resolution
Divine Right Action and Divine Right Thought
Divine Serenity
Divine Success
Divine Truth
Divine Understanding
Divine Will
Divine Wisdom
Divine Word
Power of the Miraculous

The following energies are the Highest Frequency of Energies attainable at the Human Kingdom level:

Higher Heart Consciousness (Proper Self-Love)
Proper Connection to Self
Proper Discernment
Proper Personal Power
Proper Self-Confidence
Proper Self-Responsibility

LaVergne, TN USA
07 January 2010
169049LV00001B/1/P

9 781609 100803